7/8/13
For my friend
Pat. —
Enjoy the Read
Phyllis

The Fragrance of

Lilacs

Phyllis E. Lambert

You travel the world, and come home to discover the best adventure of all was your very own childhood.

Published by Lulu Press, Inc.

Copyright@2015 by Phyllis E. Lambert

FragranceofLilacs@Gmail.com

Second printing: May 2015

ISBN Number: 978-1-312-98381-6

"Well, my book is written--let it go. But if I were only to write it over again there wouldn't be so many things left out. They burn in me; and they keep multiplying."   Mark Twain - Letter to W. D. Howells, 22 Sept 1889 (referring to A Connecticut Yankee in King Arthur's Court)

For

My Family

Please walk with me, my darlings,

through the years of my childhood,

my highs and my lows,

my joys and my sorrows.

I hope you will laugh

and I hope you will cry,

just as I have.

Acknowledgements

It is impossible for me to list the names of everyone who helped with the realization of my dream; this memoir. It has been a work in progress for many years, through countless writing classes and writing groups. Instructors, fellow writers, and friends have read the manuscript in various forms of completion and have encouraged me to document my childhood memories.

My friend, Russ Hatler, continues to provide an infinite amount of wisdom and patience, and is always available when I need his advice. This book would never have been published without his help.

And so to one and all, thank you, thank you, thank you.

Foreword

Of course I was in denial, with a capital D-E-N-I-A-L, that in the blink of the proverbial eye I would morph into an old woman. Aging happens much quicker than anyone expects. You try not to notice until one awful day you see your mother's deeply veined, time-worn hands and crooked fingers where your slim, youthful fingers used to be.

When I became a septuagenarian, I tried to come to terms with the frightening realization of growing old. Nine years later I'm still trying. I cannot stop the process, but I can document the journey. I have neither given up on the present nor the future. Living a full, reasonably contented life makes it possible to enjoy the luxury of reflection. Like riding on a train sitting backwards—I see where I've been.

Some memories simmer and pop like bubbles in boiling pudding, tiny eruptions of sweet reverie. Others are like biting into a chunk of unsweetened chocolate-- bitter and hard to swallow. Nonetheless, I am enjoying the reruns. Documenting a childhood of experiences, I am discovering, is a formidable task. I thought it would be much easier. Just when I think I'm done, I remember something else I want to share. I can't do it alone and so I turn to my alter ego, April Laine to tell the story.

I have often been caught "talking to myself." Now, as in all exposés, the truth comes out. All this time when my family thought I was talking to myself, I was having discussions with April. She is wise, has a keen imagination and will use poetic license, with my permission, to spice up the story a bit (not to excess, you understand) just enough to make it interesting. We call it creative non-fiction which is similar to smearing a small amount of Grey Poupon mustard on a bland turkey hotdog. The mustard doesn't change the hotdog; it just makes the hotdog taste better. The story line remains true; some of the details are Grey Poupon.

And so I gather my memories in little bits and pieces the same way my father gathered hay scatterings in sunny summer fields. In the end Dad had a year's supply of hay. I hope to have a book.

Few people can rely solely on memory, least of all me. Even seemingly vivid recollections become distorted over time. And so I turn to my invaluable store of diaries, letters, scrap books and photo albums. Everyone's memories are unique and valuable. After all, each of us is a "one of a kind never to be repeated" individual. That said, I am allowing myself the luxury of recollecting to my heart's content. By doing so, I return to my childhood, seeing, smelling, touching, listening, and dreaming anew; and I want to share it with you.

My memoir, "The Fragrance of Lilacs," named itself. To understand, obviously one must have lived in an area of the world where lilacs grow. I was born and grew up in Central New York State where lilacs bloom profusely for a short time every spring. Lilac bushes are tenacious. They can grow as tall as a house and live a very long time. Nearly forgotten they continue to thrive and bloom along crumbling foundations of abandoned homesteads beside dusty roads. The short-lived white, lavender or deep purple clumps of flowers consist of numerous tiny, star-shaped blossoms. To understand my affection for lilacs, you must have suffered through long, cold winters.

Every spring their transitory presence comes as a surprise. Strolling outside early in the morning when the dew is fresh you notice sweetness in the air and realize with delight that the lilacs are back. The delicate fragrance of lilacs clings gently to the morning breeze and embraces our senses like precious memories.

April and I, to the best of our ability, present the early life of a country girl named Phyllis.

Tales from the Fireside:

The Lambert's

and

The Van Dyke's

1900 – 1934

Flames dance like whirling dervishes swirling around logs in a mesmerizing kaleidoscope of colors. Stars, the ancients believed, are created from the sparks of billions and billions of campfires burning throughout the ages. Stories, too, spring to life around campfires spun from the tapestry of memories and traditions sprinkled with imagination.

Phyllis's father, Erwin was a story teller. He was particularly inspired on a late August evening in 1957 when his brother, Noah, whom he had not seen in many years, was visiting from California. As the men and their families relaxed in the glow of the campfire, Erwin's thoughts drifted with the leaping flames back to the "good

1

old days." Lambert family stories continued well into the night.

Eager to have her story told, Erwin's wife, Levina, chimed in with stories of Holland, the Van Dyke family emigration, and their life as produce farmers working rich muck land in Chittenango Station, New York

Erwin Antoine Lambert was born on Monday, January 29, 1900, in the hamlet of Philadelphia, New York, the seventh child and fifth son of Joseph and Cora Lambert. It was President McKinley's birthday. Noah was only five years old, but he remembers Erwin's birthday as cold and blustery.

Located in the harsh hinterlands of northern New York State a few miles south of the Canadian border, Philadelphia winters were long and frigid.

The Lambert saga began twelve years earlier on February 25, 1888, when Cora Stage, 16, and Joseph Lambert, 28, were married in the Methodist-Episcopal Church parsonage in Cora's hometown of Theresa, N.Y.

Cora's mother died when she was a baby, and her father died or disappeared when she was around two years old. The Duffany family, who were relatives of her mother, brought up Cora.

Joseph was born in Montebello, Quebec, Canada and moved to the United States when he was 17. French was his first language. Phyllis studies a picture of her blacksmith grandfather holding the reins of a horse. She identifies with the man with a stoic expression, a neat white mustache and large, hard-working hands.

In a list of names from Cora's family Bible, Joseph's death is listed as 1930. According to a copy of his certificate of death from the Ogdensburg City Hospital and Orphan Asylum, he died in 1935. The certificate states that he was a blacksmith for 45 years and worked in a blacksmith shop until 1925. It states that he was white

2

and married at the time of his death. Erwin claims "Old Joe" died in the poorhouse. Cora died on June 11, 1954.

We can only speculate about Cora and Joseph's life together but certainly Joe was right proud of his pretty, slim second wife when he signed his **X** on the marriage license. He was short and muscular with a stern, handsome face. Cora was soon in a family way. She gave birth to twin girls, Florence and Flora on December 27, 1889.

When Erwin was born eleven years later, we expect the scene was something like this: The twins stood next to the rocking chair where Cora held Erwin, bickering over who would be the first to hold their new brother. The blue eyed baby boy had found his mother's ample breast. Cora was satisfied that he was sucking well.

Big brother Harry, 9, was not happy about another mouth to feed. Mealtime was already slim pickings. Herbert, 7, and Noah, 5, huddled close to the potbelly coal stove in the frugal living room playing with tin toy soldiers. A tabby cat, a good mouser, was curled up close to the stove. Howard, 3, clung to the sleeve of Cora's nightgown, peering at the little brother who had taken his place as Mama's baby. Noah remembers when the doctor, carrying a black bag, made a house call proclaiming that mother and infant were doing well.

Erwin wasn't Mama's baby for long. Ernest arrived in May 1902. The sixteen-year-old twins, Florence and Flora, reacted with excitement when Gladys was born in 1905. At long last they had a sister.

When Samuel came along on July 27, 1909, Cora undoubtedly prayed earnestly, pleading with the good Lord not to send her any more bundles of joy. The twins were born when she was 17 and at age 37; ten babies later, she had to have been plumb worn out. Every day was a struggle with little money and few conveniences.

3

To say Cora had a hard life does not begin to describe the routine drudgery of her existence. She raised her family at a time when a scant ten per-cent of the rural population had electricity. Just imagine hand-washing clothes for a family of twelve. Cora had an abundant supply of elbow grease and scads of kids to help with the chores. The children were expected to work odd jobs and work they did.

During their boyhood Cora and Joseph's sons would have enjoyed hanging around a blacksmith shop watching farriers work at the flaming forge, shaping metal horse shoes to size. The boys stood on upturned wooden packing crates to reach the horses, curry-combing their sleek coats after they were shod. Customers appreciated the extra attention to their animals and occasionally gave the boys pennies. Phyllis imagines Joseph whistling while he worked, his muscular arms drenched with sweat. The muscles in his chest rippled as he lifted heavy hammers over his head, pounding steel into shape.

The Lambert kids did not have material possessions but they had fun with lots of hell-raising. It was in the good old summer time, of course, the day Erwin remembers learning to swim. He stood on a log protruding from the shore into the Indian River on a hot day when he was five and a half years old, watching the older boys swim and dunk each other. He wanted to jump, but the river looked cold and deep and he felt very small.

"Jump, jump, jump;" the big kids chided. "Scared ain't ya?"

He felt a shove from behind while he was trying to muster up the courage to jump, then cheers and laughter. Little Erwin gasped and gulped for air as he bobbed up and down in the Indian River

"Swim, swim," the big boys taunted.

4

The little boy pulled at the water desperately doggy paddling and kicking back to the log. He wasn't scared anymore.

Roaming the freight yard and pinching candy bars from open railroad cars was all-in-a-day's play. No harm done as long as Ma didn't find out, they thought, wiping chocolate off their faces. They earned pocket change working for neighbors, pushing heavy lawn mowers in the summer time and shoveling snow through six-month-long winters. The boys played hooky from school on pleasant days and picked up odd jobs to pay for treats their parents could not afford. They played baseball in vacant lots as soon as they were old enough to hold a bat. Erwin loved the game. His team was the New York Highlanders who became the New York Yankees in 1913.

Erwin rode in on the wings of the 20th Century. He liked to say he always knew his age because it was the same as the year. New inventions gradually improved living standards, and medical advances increased life expectancy. Erwin was not quite four years old when two brothers who owned a bicycle shop in Dayton, Ohio, finished a project they had been tinkering with for years. Using a sandy beach in Kitty Hawk, North Carolina, as a testing ground on December 17, 1903, the Wright Brothers took their flimsy home-made flying machine into the air in a series of flights, the longest lasting 59 seconds. People paid little attention.

"It is utter foolishness," most folks scoffed; "nothing will come of it."

Henry Ford's gasoline powered horseless carriage, the Model T, left the factory in 1908 when Erwin was in second grade. Most people thought the term "horse power" meant just that, but times were changing. It would be a long time before Erwin saw one of the smelly Tin

Lizzies and many more years would pass before he actually owned an automobile.

Phyllis's maternal grandparents, Willem Cornelius VanDyke and Maria Maatje Schoonen, were married in Tholen, Holland, on May 20, 1903. Levina Herminia, was born on June 5, 1905. The baby had brown eyes, dark hair and porcelain white skin. Maatje held the new born lovingly to her breast, but Willem scowled in disappointment. He twisted his mustache as he stared at the little girl. They already had one daughter, Marie. This child was meant to be a son.

By the time their son, Marinus, was born two years later, Willem was restless. He heard amazing stories about the land of prosperity across the ocean. Friends had immigrated to the United States and urged him to join them. Shy Maatje, the sensible wife, was heart-broken about the plans to leave their native Holland. Her husband had a decent job as a traveling gramophone salesman, but Willem was the boss and his mind was made up. He felt certain he would prosper in America when he sailed in early 1912 to join his countrymen who had settled in Central New York State. His family would follow in late November of that year whether they wanted to or not. When the time came, the children carried blocks of wood to the shoe-maker who carved new shoes for the trip, but the shoes disappeared off the hearth. Maatje's mother, whom the children called "Oma," admitted to the theft.

"It is all I will have left of them," she said crying. "They can wear their leather Sunday shoes."

The S.S. Noordam, a Holland America ship, sailed out of Rotterdam on November 30, 1912, bound for New York City. As Maatje hustled her excited children on to the ship, she felt only sadness knowing she would never see her family again.

Maatje was pathetically seasick and spent most of the voyage curled up on the comforting feather tick she brought from home. Marie, 8, Levina, 7, and Marinus, 4, roamed the ship on their own, peering over the rails of the huge ship at the wild, cold Atlantic. Everything was confusing. Unfamiliar food was served in the dining room. They had never seen or heard of bananas, and they hated the taste of the strange fruit.

"I still don't like them," Levina said as she recalled the story.

The little family was frightened, bewildered and desperately homesick when they arrived at Ellis Island on December 12, 1912. It was Maatje's 35th birthday. They did not speak a word of English and were confused by the babble of languages inside the massive immigration depot. Willem sent a man they did not know to meet them with only a small picture of Maatje for identification. Somehow, Maatje felt it was by the grace of God, they found each other in the cavernous registry room. For the first time since they had left the Netherlands, her panic subsided. Soon she would see Willem.

They traveled 300 miles west by train from New York City to Chittenango Station, a rural area in the center of New York State near Oneida Lake. Willem had purchased a piece of rich farmland called muck, on time, where he raised vegetables. Willem and his children peddled sweet corn, tomatoes, cucumbers, squash, potatoes, celery, and onions with a horse and wagon. Summer residents around Oneida Lake looked forward every week to the Van Dyke's fresh vegetables.

Maatje and her children suffered from a skin disease inherited from her side of the family that caused their tender skin to break and bruise easily. Knees were always sore, and fingers were skinned from many hours of hard work pulling weeds on hands and knees in the black earth.

7

Rag bandages were tied around the children's bruised, blistered and raw knees, knuckles, ankles, shins, and elbows. Despite the hardships, they found camaraderie in the fields working with other immigrants.

"Unbelieveable things happened," Levina said, "like the day I watched an Italian woman give birth in the field."

The children found arrowheads and bits of pottery while weeding onions in the rich black earth and stashed the treasures in their pockets. At the time they were unaware of the Oneida Indians, a tribe in the Iroquois Confederacy who had inhabited the area.

That fall Levina and Marie were placed in first grade until they learned the English language. Bright girls, they learned quickly and advanced to higher grades. They helped their father learn English, but Maatje was not interested. Dutch was her language.

Willem built a sturdy two-story wood frame house for his family on several acres of scrub land a few miles from his acre of muck. Huckleberry bushes flourished on his land and Willem added fresh berries to his offerings. Having her own house made Maatje a little happier but not much. She never stopped missing Holland and the family and friends she had left behind.

The long, straight road across the flats of Chittenango Station from the Free Methodist Church to the Van Dyke home glowed in the light of a full moon. Marie, Levina, and Marinus held hands as they walked tentatively through the stark landscape with muck land lining both sides of the road. Their raving pastor preached hellfire and brimstone at the church youth meeting. It was the same theme on Sunday mornings.

"*Repent,*" he bellowed. "*In the name of the Lord, repent.*"

Marie, Levina, Marinus,

Willem and Maatje

The children repented, but they still expected to be scooped up any minute by the devil's henchman because they were fearful they had not been good enough. They prayed silently, thanking God for the moonlight that made the long walk home easier. Maatje would be waiting anxiously at the door.

Levina's intransigent father pulled his daughters out of school in 1918.

"Eighth grade enough for girls," he said in broken English. His son, Marinus, however, was allowed to finish high school. The girls cried and begged, but their father stood firm, pointing his finger in determination and twisting his bushy moustache for emphasis.

"It time you go work," he insisted, as though crawling on their hands and knees across the muck weeding vegetables was not work.

Willem made arrangements for his daughters to work for Mr. Stanley Bittner. When the school term was over, Levina and Marie began their careers as dairy maids for the local entrepreneur who owned a large dairy farm and a grist mill in Chittenango Station.

Levina cried herself to sleep many nights, still holding fast to her dream of becoming a school teacher. She told Mr. Bittner about her hopes for the future, although she knew she should not have mentioned it. Meanwhile the girls milked and milked and milked, twice a day, six days a week.

Even before Levina's tearful admission that she wanted more than anything to be a school teacher, Mr. Bittner had recognized her intelligence. He encouraged Levina's father, who he called Billy, to allow his girls to finish school. The answer was always, "*Nee, nee, nee.*"

"PROHIBITION PASSED" was splashed across the top of newspapers in banner headlines when the United States took on "The Noble Experiment." With the passage of the 18th Amendment to the Constitution in 1919, the selling, creating, and moving of alcoholic beverages was made illegal in the U.S. The amendment that was intended to lessen the "evils" of alcohol created new problems instead. Organized crime escalated, and notorious names such as Al Capone appeared. Speakeasies, private clubs for the illegal sale of alcohol, sprang up all across the nation.

The Roaring Twenties were boom years in the United States. Henry Ford cranked out automobiles, and radios were becoming commonplace. In 1927 "The Jazz Singer" starring Al Jolson, triggered the talking-picture revolution. "The War to End all Wars" had been fought and won; times were good. A wave of optimism spread across the country. People took hard-earned money out of savings accounts and speculated in get-rich-quick schemes.

Shredded Wheat

Erwin (L) and his younger brother, Ernest, nursed a Lambert trait called "terminal wanderlust." They were in their twenties when they left northern New York blazing the Lambert Trail to California. Visions of vast good fortune danced in their impressionistic minds. Compared to their birthplace in the cold northeast, southern California was paradise. Erwin maintained that belief to his dying day. The brothers worked for the Shredded Wheat Company in Compton dubbing themselves "The Shredded Wheat Twins."

They had jobs, girlfriends, and good times. Erwin did not talk much about his girlfriend, Juanita. He got the impression from letters that his family was not thrilled about his relationship. Perhaps Juanita's south-of-the-border sounding name was the problem. It did not seem important to Erwin. After all, his family lived 3,000 miles away. It was not long before Ernest and Erwin were married men.

"Being single was just a happy memory," Erwin said wistfully.

By the summer of 1920, despite their father's continuing opposition, Stanley Bittner made arrangements for the Van Dyke girls to move to Ithaca, New York, where he found them jobs as live-in mothers' helpers while they attended high school. Levina worked for the Weatherby family.

Willem Van Dyke was not speaking to his daughters on the August day when Mr. Bittner picked them up for the 70-mile drive to Ithaca. Maatje was broken-hearted to see them leave home although she held back her tears. After they got in the car, Levina realized she had forgotten her hat. Returning to the house she found her mother sobbing. As they drove south along Route 13, Levina counted the Burgess Clothing signs that were painted on the sides of barns. She was consoled, knowing she would be able to find her way home by following the signs.

The 1920's began in hope and euphoria and ended in despair. The stock market peaked in September 1929. Stocks were so high no one was buying.

On October 24, 1929, more stocks were sold than were purchased, causing the market to plummet. By October 29, the day dubbed "Black Tuesday," the decline caused a panic. The Great Stock Market Crash signaled the beginning of the Great Depression.

"Prosperity is just around the corner," President Hoover promised the nation, but his attempts to stimulate the economy failed. Twenty-five percent of the U. S. population was unemployed. Erwin hung on, picking up odd jobs. He particularly enjoyed a stint on a chicken ranch, and dreamed of having one of his own..

Erwin usually looked on the bright side of life and whistled his way through all kinds of problems. As if the dire economy was not bad enough, Erwin's marriage broke up. It was something he did not talk about. Erwin roamed around southern California, drifting from job to job, uncertain what to do next.

Levina was in her twenties by the time she graduated from high school. She was accepted at Cornell University but dropped out after two semesters because she was not willing to wait another three years to become a teacher. Finding another way, she attended Skaneateles Training Class, a 12-month teachers' certification course and returned home to teach grades one through eight in a one-room school in Chittenango Falls. Her father Willem, who his friends called Billy, did not outright apologize, but he certainly changed his tune.

"That my girl," he said with pride "that teacher up there, that my girl."

Marie married Fred Olmsted soon after returning home from Ithaca. Levina married Fred's brother, George, on August 20, 1929. The Olmsted Brothers worked their own dairy farms and the future looked bright, but living happily ever after was not as easy as they had expected.

In 1932, the American electorate voted President Herbert Hoover out of office, hoping for an end to nationwide economic chaos and unemployment. Franklin D. Roosevelt, a Democrat, took his presidential oath in January 1933 affirming to the nation: "The only thing we have to fear is fear itself." President Roosevelt initiated his New Deal programs that stimulated the economy and gave people hope.

Although Erwin was unaware that destiny was at work, he decided one afternoon in 1934 when he was between jobs, that it was time to visit the folks back home in central New York. Erwin's sister, Florence Howard, a widow, owned Howard's Restaurant in Chittenango.

"I'll be back," he told Ernie.

Erwin worked his way slowly eastward making an adventure of the trip and supporting himself with day jobs. He was especially proud of the time he spent working on the Hoover Dam project. Also known as Boulder Dam, the arch-gravity concrete dam spans the Black Canyon of the Colorado River on the border between Arizona and Nevada. When it was completed in

1935, it was the world's largest power-producing plant and the world's largest concrete structure.

One stormy winter afternoon in 1934, Levina Olmsted dismissed her students early and left the school where she taught, anxious to get home before the snow storm worsened. Turning off the main road, she made her way cautiously along the narrow dirt road bordering Chittenango Creek that lead to their farm. The farm house she shared with her husband was located on one side of the road and the barn was on the other. She parked her Model T by the barn because the hill leading to the house was steep and slippery. Plodding through swirling snow to the house, she climbed gingerly up icy steps to the wide front porch. Opening the door, she cleared her throat, as she often did.

"George, I'm home," she called to her husband. She took off her hat and draped her coat over a chair near a coal fire blazing in a pot belly stove in the living room. She could smell the heat from the hot metal stove and was thankful to be home where it was warm.

"George?" She heard a noise in the bedroom that was separated from the living room by heavy draperies hanging across the doorway. Pushing back the draperies she was stunned to see her husband scrambling off the bed pulling up his trousers. He was not alone.

Levina had suspected George was cheating on her earlier in the year when she was in the hospital for the removal of a diseased ovary. People talk and Levina's friends were no exception. Something was going on between George and Elsie, they whispered. She gave him the benefit of the doubt, but now, in one crushing moment her worst fears were confirmed.

Confused and sobbing, she left the house and headed north on the slippery, curvy, snow-covered road high above the creek heading toward Chittenango. Suddenly, as though someone had yanked the steering wheel, her car went into a skid and careened off the road. Two small trees part way down the steep ravine caught the car and kept her black Ford from crashing into cold, dark Chittenango creek. She felt a crushing blow to her face breaking her nose and gashing her forehead as the car struck trees just above the creek. Bruised and bloodied, sobbing and praying, "Oh dear Lord, oh dear Lord," she crawled up the steep, snow-covered embankment to the road and made her way to the closest house for help.

Vi, as her friends called her, prayed about her situation, pulled herself together and moved back home with her father. (Maatje, Levina's mother, had died of stomach cancer in 1933 on her 56th birthday).

Levina loved her teaching job but she needed more money. Her marriage was in ruins, her car was wrecked and more than anything, she needed to keep busy.

Walking along Genesee Street in Chittenango on an early spring day, she noticed a "Help Wanted" sign in the window of Howard's Restaurant. Florence Howard and Levina knew each other, but then most people in Chittenango knew each other. Levina said she could only work part-time until school closed for the summer.

"The job is yours, honey," Florence said smiling through thick spectacles at the pretty young woman. "Can you start tomorrow?"

One - 1934-1935

**Howard's Restaurant
Genesee Street,
Chittenango, New York**

"The old burgh hasn't changed much," Erwin thought as he stepped out of his Model T Ford in front of Howard's Restaurant early on a June morning in 1934. There were more jalopies parked along Genesee Street, but everything else looked pretty much the same as when he had left a decade or more earlier.

Standing back on the old sod, all he had to show for his time out west was a second-hand Tin Lizzie. He was out of a job, and had worked his way clear across the country to visit his family. He didn't plan to stay long.

"Hey big Sis," he said in his jovial manner as he swung through the door of the restaurant, "How about a cup of Java?"

"Hello kid." Florence stepped out from behind the counter, and pressed him to her ample bosom. "How's my handsome little brother?" She was expecting him.

"Do I see gray hair?" he teased. At 45 she was his eldest sibling.

"Nope." She tucked a lock of black hair under her hair net, smoothed her light blue uniform, adjusted her spectacles, and said emphatically, "Haven't aged a day."

Erwin sat at one of the tables near a window facing the street, savoring a big breakfast; bacon, eggs sunny side up, toast, jam, and a fried cake.

"You eat a lot for a little guy," Florence, teased. "Just feeding your gumption, I expect."

"How's business?" Erwin asked, hoping for short-term employment.

"Well, everybody has to eat," Florence quipped handing him a white apron. "Too bad I don't fancy the restaurant business."

When Florence's second husband Lester "Doc" Howard died in 1931, she was, to use her words, "stuck with it."

Erwin poured himself a second cup of coffee and unfolded the newspaper. He kept up-to-date on world news, politics and the New York Yankees. He read the headline aloud: ***"Hitler and Mussolini to Meet in Venice, Italy."*** Adolf Hitler had been appointed Chancellor of Germany in 1933, and with President von Hindenburg in poor health, he had usurped more and more power.

"That Hitler's one damn shrewd politician." Erwin butted his cigarette, folded the newspaper and picked up the apron. It was time to sling hash.

The bell over the door announced the arrival of customers, and Erwin greeted each one in his melodious Bing Crosby imitation as he poured coffee into heavy, white china mugs. When the breakfast crowd had left, Florence and Erwin chatted as they cleaned up the dining room.

"Just wait 'til you see Levina, my new cook. She's as pretty as a picture, and twice as smart." Florence lifted her eyebrows for emphasis. "She teaches at the little school up in Chittenango Falls."

"Why's she working here if she's a teacher?"

"She's ambitious and she needs to pay for a divorce from her cheating husband. She caught them in the act last winter right in her own marriage bed."

Levina would have been humiliated if she knew what Florence had said. She did not air her dirty laundry in public.

The evening was warm. Erwin and Levina sat at a picnic table behind the restaurant next to Chittenango Creek getting acquainted. The popular trout stream babbled along between wooded banks flowing north toward Oneida Lake as the two lingered over coffee.

"Listen to the creek," Levina said. "It is singing."

Erwin lit up a Camel cigarette and blew out the match. He was a prolific storyteller and was soon weaving lavish tales about life in California, and his drive back east working day jobs as he went along.

"I'm damn proud to have worked on Boulder Dam," he said taking a long puff from his cigarette, and blowing smoke through his nose. "That is some hunk of cement." He glanced at Levina who was studying her hands, and sizing him up. *He's probably a heart breaker with his California tan, black hair, nice teeth and blue eyes, she thought.*

"I'm not staying here long; just wanted to see Ma and the gang. When I go back, I'm gonna get myself a little chicken ranch."

"I couldn't do that," Levina said, "I'm too much of a home body. I'm a school teacher at Chittenango Falls." She glanced at Erwin for his reaction.

"Yeah, so Flo said. Which grades do you teach?"

"All eight grades. I love teaching. Even back in Holland before we emigrated, I played school with my dolls. Mother was furious when father pulled my sister and me out of school after eighth grade and found us jobs as dairy maids. I was over 20 before I graduated high school in Ithaca, but that's another story. I earned my teaching certificate in twelve months at the Skaneateles Teachers' Training Class."

"Wow! All eight grades." Erwin took another puff and gazed at Levina through a veil of smoke. *Yessiree,* he thought, *there is one good looking woman.* He didn't realize it then, but his California days were gone for good.

"I need a vacation," Florence announced one July morning, "a well-deserved vacation. Do you two think you could handle the business for a while?"

"Sure thing," Erwin said. "This is as good a place as any to spend the summer."

He was in no hurry to get back to California.

20

Naturally affable, he relished the hands-on, people-oriented restaurant business. Levina loved the work, and was glad to have the extra hours.

The couple could not have been happier. Levina was itching to deep clean the restaurant, and just as soon as Florence walked out the door, the Dutch in Levina got busy. She disinfected everything, and scrubbed the wood floor on her hands and knees, while Erwin painted the dining room.

"I've seen your sister flick mold off pie before serving it," Levina scoffed. "And cook up rank steaks I wouldn't serve to a dog."

There would be no more of that nonsense while Erwin and Levina were in charge. Levina was a good cook and everything was served fresh. Erwin had a delightful smile and a friendly demeanor, singing and whistling while he worked. Levina's daily blue plate specials and her scrumptious pies sold out day after day. Business picked up and Howard's Restaurant flourished the summer of '34.

Romance blossomed and the new sweethearts were having the time of their lives, working hard, dreaming big dreams and planning to tie the knot as soon as Levina's divorce was final. Knowing there was no love lost between Florence and the restaurant, it made sense to assume she would be happy to sell the business to them. Working long hours they made Howard's the most popular restaurant in Chittenango. Florence phoned from time to time asking how things were going.

"I can come back early if you need me," she said.

"Have a good time, everything is hunky dory," Erwin assured his big sister. "We have plenty of help. Ma and Frank have a tent set up out back by the creek."

Erwin teased his mother, Cora, and Frank, her second husband, calling them "kissing cousins." Erwin wasn't kidding. Frank and Cora were first cousins.

"Oh he makes me feel so good," Cora told Levina whose face flushed bright red when she heard what Cora said.

"Cora acts like a love-sick fool," Levina confided to her sister, Marie, whom she visited every week.

"What's the matter?" Marie asked. "Are you jealous?"

"She's old enough to know better. You'd think they were newlyweds. There's a time and a place for everything," Levina sputtered. She did not approve of public displays of affection.

"No!" Florence said adamantly when she got home. "This restaurant is not for sale! How would you pay for it anyway? Have you thought about that?" Florence's thick spectacles gave her a bug-eyed look. A determined woman, she stood her ground. Levina listened in disbelief as Florence's harsh words shattered their dreams. Grabbing her purse, she dashed out of the restaurant in tears.

Erwin needed a job. Central New York was dairy country. Small farms dotted every picturesque hill and dale. He knew next to nothing about dairy cows, but being his own boss appealed to him.

"Always wished I had a chicken ranch," Erwin said more than once. What he really wanted was to take Levina back to California.

"If wishes were horses, beggars would ride," Levina retorted, and that was that.

Erwin was in love, so he made the best of it. His brother, Herb, owned a dairy farm on Perryville Road just south of Chittenango, and Erwin offered to work all winter for room and board to cut his dairy farming teeth. By April he had a loan from Production Credit, rented a farm, and went into debt for a small herd of Holsteins and used equipment. He had no problem putting his nose to the grindstone.

Two – 1935-1937

The Lamberts

Erwin Lambert and Levina VanDyke were married on May 3, 1935, in the First Baptist Church Parsonage in Watertown, N.Y. Erwin's younger sister Gladys, and her husband Ferdinand, who lived in Watertown, stood up with them. The newlyweds spent a two-day honeymoon on the St. Lawrence River not far from Philadelphia, New York where Erwin grew up. It would be eleven years before they took another day off.

Temperatures that July were above average, as though the summer was making up for a frigid winter and a cold, wet spring. The Lamberts were up every day before the rooster crowed at dawn, and went to bed with the chickens at dusk.

"It's a damn good hay day," Erwin said on a hot afternoon. Removing his sweaty blue denim cap for a moment, he wiped his damp brow with a big red and black plaid handkerchief. A good hay day was hot and dry. Erwin mowed tall, ripe timothy and alfalfa grasses, and when it was dry he hooked the horses to the dump rake to form rows of rolled hay called windrows.

When it was time to load hay, Levina drove the team of horses standing at the front of the wagon and Erwin pulled the hay from the loader at the rear. The ravenous slant-shaped hay loader looked like a wide playground slide with two large wheels. It towered above the wagon and appeared to be gobbling up hay with long, sharp metal teeth attached to revolving belts. The machine shuddered, rattled, and spewed dust into the air that stuck to Erwin's sweaty face and arms.

At first the fragrant hay fell down off the loader onto the wagon as Erwin fashioned firm, even loads. As the load grew higher, Levina and Erwin moved up with the hay. When the wagon was full, the top of the loader was even with the load of hay. Levina, who started out staring

24

at horses' rumps, was in the end looking down on the team.

When the equipment failed, as it often did, Erwin expressed his displeasure by christening whichever object had broken down with rude names such as "sonofabitch!" or "freakin' so and so." Raised in a strict Free Methodist Church, cuss words grated on Levina's sensibilities. She grimaced at every blasphemous word, but she didn't complain that first year.

The rented farm where they lived was nestled against a pretty wooded hillside in view of Chittenango Creek. The trout stream, the size of a small river, began at Cazenovia Lake and plunged 167 feet over ancient bedrock ledges of Chittenango Falls. It rushed on north past the Lambert's toward Chittenango emptying into Oneida Lake at the foothills of the Adirondack Mountains.

The upstairs bedroom windows were open and a welcome late July breeze drifted in from across the creek. Erwin was exhausted after a very long, hard-working day. He collapsed buck-naked on top of the clean, white sheet, his dark hair uncombed and still wet from his bath.

Levina, a living cliché, tidied up her kitchen before going to bed. There was a place for everything and everything was in its place. She walked carefully down steep wooden stairs, and placed milk, butter and eggs on stones in a stream of icy cold spring water that flowed through the cellar. They didn't own an ice box. Levina loved the pleasant dampness and the earthy smell, so like the muck land where she had worked in her father's vegetable plot after the family emigrated from Holland in 1912.

When her work was done, she climbed the stifling hot enclosed stairway to the bedroom, carrying a glass kerosene lamp because there was no electricity. She placed the lamp carefully on the night stand and blew out the flame. A faint sweet odor of burning wick and kerosene clung to the air.

Wearing a thin, cotton nightgown, fragrant and soft from the clothes line, she sighed as she crawled into bed next to her husband. It had been over two months since their wedding day and she longed to be pregnant. She was 30 and Erwin was 35. There was no time to waste. Gently, she pulled the top sheet over them, her body brushing against his. Rousing, he felt the fullness of her breasts. The gentle summer breeze ruffled the cream-colored tulle curtains in a seductive dance.

After making love, the couple lay close together on damp sheets, sweaty and contented. Erwin drifted back to sleep. Levina remained awake, unaware that her prayers had been answered, and a new life had begun. She was lulled to sleep by nature's melody where tiny peeper frogs and myriad insects along the creek performed an evening symphony.

Summer's greenery was overcome by the first killing frost; garden vegetables were harvested, corn stalks hung lifeless in helpless submission to the changing seasons. Indian summer teased with a warm spell. It was Autumn's last curtain call before winter. A year's supply of cord wood was stacked along the house and on the front porch. The barn was packed with fragrant hay, and the silo was nearly full of chopped corn silage. The corn crib overflowed with firm, golden ears, and farm cats guarded the treasure feasting on field mice they found hiding beneath the ears of corn.

Levina stood on the side lawn marveling at autumn colors ablaze on the hillside. She was entering her third month of pregnancy and was anxious to feel some sign of life. Gently caressing her tummy, Levina whispered her son's name, "John Rodney, John Rodney" like a lullaby.

Erwin rode on the metal seat of the corn harvester in a nearby field holding the reins to his team of dusty brown work horses. Levina watched and waved as the horses pulled the machine along the edge of the field capturing one row of corn at a time in a vice-like grip. The machine bundled and tied the cornstalks and ejected them on the ground. Erwin later picked up the bundles with a pitch fork and tossed them on a wagon that was pulled by the horses to the silo. There was no end to the back-breaking work.

A power take-off wheel attached to the side of the McCormick Deering 1020 tractor was fitted with a heavy canvas belt that whirled unsteadily, powering the voracious silo filler that was set up next to the silo. Silo filling was dangerous work. It worried Levina and she prayed daily for her husband's safety. Jimmy, a young man who lived on Perryville Road, had been killed earlier that year after his jacket sleeve was snagged in the moving machinery and his arm was severed, leaving a wife and baby boy. Erwin carefully guided one bundle at a time through the groaning machine. Powerful, piercing blades pulverized the corn stalks that were propelled up a metal cylinder into the silo with a swooshing sound: chop–swoosh, chop–swoosh. In the natural order of things, the chopped corn generated heat in the silo as it fermented, cooked. and was preserved. The cows ate it ravenously.

Quart mason jars of home-canned tomatoes, string beans, applesauce, peaches, bread and butter pickles and pickled beets filled cellar shelves. The root cellar held potatoes, carrots, onions, cabbage and winter squash. A hog was slaughtered, and fragrant hams and bacon hung from the smokehouse ceiling. Levina canned tender chunks of pork and made spicy country sausage and head cheese that she packed in earthenware crocks sealed with lard. The feisty rooster with colorful plumage watched over his harem of free-ranging hens that produced eggs with deep yellow yolks.

Winter was the only season when Erwin had spare time. He repaired farm equipment and worked around the house and barn to keep the place looking neat. After morning chores, he read the newspaper and briefed his wife as she busied herself around the kitchen.

From time to time, Levina made soap with three simple ingredients: lard, lye, and water. The cream-colored laundry soap had a fresh smell, and bore no resemblance to lard or lye. She listened to Erwin with one ear as she cut the cooled, hardened soap into chunks with a butcher knife. She used her soap for washing clothes, but they bought Ivory soap for their baths.

"The Nazi Party activists have initiated a major wave of assaults, vandalism, and boycotts against German Jews," Erwin read. "Poor buggers," he said shaking his head in disbelief. He didn't always trust shifty Jewish businessmen, but they did not deserve what the Nazi's were dishing out.

The Nuremberg Laws of 1935 were denaturalization laws passed in Germany that used a pseudoscientific basis for racial discrimination against Jews and other non-Aryans. The whole world would soon witness the blight of Hitler's destructive domination. Erwin and Levina would bring their baby into a world that was on the brink of a second world war.

Levina's sister, Marie, came to call on Christmas Day with her sons, five-year-old Kenny, four-year-old Jerry and Grandpa Van Dyke. Levina and Marie took turns visiting their widowed father biweekly, taking food and helping with house work. It was the first time he had been to the Lambert home. Brightly wrapped packages were piled under the cedar tree that Erwin had cut in the swamp and Levina had decorated. After a succulent roast pork dinner, everyone opened gifts, and Erwin took Grandpa to the barn to show off his dairy cows.

"I have a feeling you'll have a girl," Marie told her sister as the boys wrestled on the wood plank floor, "a nice, quiet little girl." Levina didn't want to hear that.

Suddenly, Jerry grabbed his elbow screaming in pain. Both boys had inherited the Schoonen family tender skin, and were always bunged up. Their elbows and fingers were wrapped in blood-stained rag bandages. Levina, Marie, their brother Marinus and his two children Bernice and Wesley, all had the disease.

"Oh dear," Levina gasped, "he's hurt himself again."

"Boys will be boys," Marie said.

Levina prayed every night that her own child would be spared the dreaded disease. She couldn't bear to think of her son with sores, bruises and blisters disfiguring his little body. Marie didn't notice her sister's tears as she grabbed Kenny and wrestled him into his coat.

(Years later when Kenneth was drafted into the U.S. Army, the disease was diagnosed as Dystrophic Epidermolysis Bullosa, known as EB. He was given a medical discharge.)

"If only Florence had sold us the restaurant," Levina opined as she helped Marie pick Jerry up off the floor. "She was just jealous because Erwin and I were making a success of the business. Farming is a bitter uphill battle. I fear it will be the death of us." *(Florence ultimately sold the restaurant, and Levina never completely forgave her).* Also a farmer's wife, Marie knew the familiar story all too well, but she never complained.

Levina's spirits lifted as the weather improved. By mid-April most of the snow had melted except for a few patches lingering in the woods and along the creek. The sun was bright the day Erwin drove his wife 30 miles to Syracuse Memorial Hospital.

"This sunshine reminds me of good old Southern California," he said wistfully.

"It's beautiful here too," Levina said. "We must bloom where we are planted."

Levina's friend, Julia who lived in Syracuse with her husband Arthur, met them at the hospital. Erwin had to hurry back home for chores.

On Tuesday, April 21, 1936, at 12:20 p.m., a 7 lb. 13 oz. baby girl was born to Erwin and Levina Lambert delivered by Dr. Schuenick and Dr. Van Ness. The nurses were Miss Skinner and Miss Johnson. According to Levina's entry in the pink baby book with gold lettering, Phyllis Elaine did not have much hair.

"When Phyllis was two days old Levina noticed her tiny heel was skinned. Nurse Skinner said it was nothing to worry about, but Levina knew better. Her baby had the dreaded skin disease.

"Phyllis has the tender skin condition, Erwin," Levina said with tears in her eyes.

"I wouldn't worry about it," Erwin said.

"Easy enough for you to say," Levina quipped. She would worry about her baby every day.

"It is a shame," said Aunt Marie, "but certainly not the end of the world."

Erwin brought his little family home on Sunday, May 3, all the more special since

it was their first wedding anniversary. If Levina was disappointed about the sex of their child, she did not let on. She had copied a poem on the first page of the baby book before Phyllis was born that ended: *"For God gave to me a baby, and I made for Him a man."* On the inside cover across from the first poem, the new mother added: *"Oh you precious little pearl and I made for Him a girl."*
\\

By coincidence, the rented farm was just down the country road from where Levina had lived with her first husband, George, and where George now lived with his new wife, Elsie

George and Elsie's first child, Shirley, was born shortly after Phyllis. As youngsters, the girls decided they must be relatives. How could they not be? Shirley's father had been married to Phyllis's mother. They weren't sure whether they were half-sisters or cousins. Either way, they were friends.

Levina and George were members of Chittenango Grange. In fact, they had been married at the grange hall. The grange is a fraternal order that lobbies for farmers' rights at state and national levels. Interested in politics, and now a farmer himself, the grange appealed to Erwin, and that first winter he requested membership. The members voted by placing a white marble in a box if they approved, and a black marble if they disapproved of the new member. There were no "black balls," and Erwin became a member of Chittenango Grange. The Lamberts and the Olmsted's socialized at grange meetings, and George and Erwin were occasional drinking buddies.

"There's nothing like a fine "seegar," Erwin said lighting up his weekly White Owl cigar; "unless it's taking a nice, Sunday drive."

31

Sunday afternoon drives were very much in vogue, but

Levina believed driving around with no particular place to go was a frivolous waste of time. As always, she had a lot to do, but she acquiesced because she was anxious to show off their baby girl. They hit the road, stopping to see this friend and that friend where they sat on broad front porches sipping iced tea, and trading gossip. Everyone said the baby was adorable. Relaxing with friends was rare, and all too soon it was chore time.

"It's getting late," Erwin said. "The old bolognas will be looking for me." The Lambert family headed home in high spirits.

"Where the hell are they?" Erwin felt a wave of panic when his cows were not waiting in the barn yard. Something was wrong. He saw the trampled down barbed wire fence as soon as he got out of the car. What he found was unimaginable. Most of his Holsteins that had been healthy that morning lay bloated on their sides in the oat field. Frantic, he ran back to the car yelling for his wife.

"Levina, Levina, the cows are sick. I'm going to Palmer's to call the vet." Palmer Brown and his wife were their closest neighbors.

"Oh dear Lord," Levina sobbed. "Why, God? Why?"

The herd had gorged on tender oat plants, munching on the delicacy for several hours that Sunday afternoon. Bellies full, they plopped down in the field chewing their cuds. The dense, green plants they had eaten produced large amounts of foam and flatulence that collected in their rumens and could not be expelled.

"Pasture bloat," the vet explained. "is a gastro condition that's most deadly in lactating animals."

The veterinarian made small ruminal fistulas in the left flanks of several young heifers, releasing the flatulence. They would survive, but it was too late for most of the herd.

"The gas puts immense pressure on the esophagus and stricken animals can't breathe," he said. "I'm very sorry."

"What the hell am I gonna do now?" Erwin felt as though someone had kicked him in the gut. "They aren't even paid for."

"We need a place where I can have an electric fence," Erwin told Levina that evening, "And then that damn bitch that first broke through would have been stopped."

The loss of their herd was devastating but it was only a temporary setback. As soon as their crops were harvested, the resilient, determined Lamberts rented a farm a few miles to the west near Eagle Village that was wired for electricity. Friends helped with the move; a ragtag parade of used farm equipment and hand-me-down home furnishings. At the Eagle Village farm, men swigged well-earned bottles of beer while the ladies prepared a smorgasbord of healthy vittles.

"Thanks everybody," Erwin said. "Here's to a new start, and good old Lambert gumption."

"I'll drink to that," someone yelled. Beer bottles clunked together in a simultaneous toast to the indomitable Lamberts.

Three – 1937-1939

Spring dragged its delicate feet in central New York, but

Bowser and Phyllis

when winter lost its grip, and the days grew mild, new grass transformed the sullen fields to a joyful green. The cows were free to roam the lush pasture between morning and night milking times. Barn work was easier, but field work was intense.

When the snow was finally gone, and the fields were dry enough to work, Erwin grasped the long wooden handles of his plow consisting of a V-shape steel blade mounted on a wooden frame. Somehow he mustered the will and energy to walk every square foot of his cultivated land with leather reins tied around his waist as the horses strained against rocky soil. Walking on plowed ground was tough and exhausting work. Watching rich dirt fold over like waves, furrow after furrow and acre after acre, Erwin managed to keep the rows of newly-plowed earth

34

perfectly straight.   He planted oats and corn every year. Hay fields needed to be reseeded every few years.

Phyllis sat in a borrowed wicker baby buggy parked at the end of the field as her father trudged behind the plow. His ankle-high work shoes were encased in mud, making it arduous to walk. Levina had brought her husband a cup of coffee. He was thankful for the break. Stretching his back, he eyed his handiwork with satisfaction.

"Thanks, Ma," he said, and turned to his daughter. "Hey, Babe." He tickled Phyllis under her chubby chin making her giggle, and squinted at the field he was working. "Gotta get out the stone boat."

Each year a new crop of stones surfaced as though the earth in Erwin's fields was filled with rocks straight down to hell.   Loose stones were lifted and loaded by hand to a flat horse-drawn stone boat.   Chains were clamped around huge boulders and dragged to the edge of the fields with the cumbersome, steel-wheeled 1020 tractor and fashioned into crude stone walls that lined the hedgerows.

When the good old summertime arrived, Erwin sang and whistled familiar tunes as he worked through long, hot days in the fields. Neighbors heard him singing thinking what a happy man he must be.

"God Bless America," he raised his voice to the heavens. "Land That I love." The song was a favorite of popular soloist, Kate Smith, whom Erwin heard on the radio when he visited the Hale family farm located up the hill from their place on Hale Road. The Lamberts didn't own a radio.

Phyllis loved hot summer days, running around naked after her bath and playing slippery eel with her mother. It was fun pulling out of the towel and hiding. Often she managed to escape the house altogether. Levina played the game every time, chasing after her daughter when she escaped outside. Phyllis invariably ran to the side of the road, patting her tummy and flaunting her nakedness.

"No, no," her mother reprimanded her spunky daughter. "No, no," she cautioned, picking up her errant child and whisking her into the house. "We do not run around in our birthday suits."

Phyllis scampered into the living room and crawled up on the couch. She was engrossed in examining her private parts when Levina came looking for her

"No, no," her mother admonished. "You mustn't play with your oopullteeoo. Nice little girls don't touch themselves down there." Levina had a vocabulary all her own.

By the time Phyllis was three Levina was happily pregnant, praying they would get their boy. Phyllis told everyone who visited she was going to get a brudder baby, but it wasn't to be. The bleeding started late one evening after Phyllis was tucked into bed. Erwin telephoned Dr. Boyd from a neighbor's house, but by the time the doctor arrived, Levina had miscarried. He attended to the hysterical Levina and then examined the perfectly formed little fetus. Erwin stared at the floor, shaking his head when Dr. Boyd said the baby was male. In the bedroom, Levina cried herself to sleep.

The bright, sunny days of Phyllis's third summer transitioned into autumn's brilliant pallet of colors. Seemingly the season was as reluctant as the people to wade through another six months of winter. Phyllis straddled her father's shoulders as he plodded along the muddy dirt path from the weathered wood frame cow barn to the house. Her buddy, Bowser, a collie mix, ran ahead, and scratched his claws down gouges on the back door where the paint was worn off. His bushy tail kept time as he waited. Levina opened the door, and Bowser squeezed into the warm farmhouse ahead of the people.

Erwin lifted his daughter off his shoulders in a swooping motion that made her giggle.

"There you go, Babe," he said with a smile in his voice. Levina gazed lovingly at her little girl as she knelt down to remove her coat, hat, mittens, and knee-high rubber boots. Supper was ready.

"I paid what I could of the bills," Levina said as they ate. "As much as I hate to admit it, the rest will just have to wait." More often than not, Levina could only pay creditors a portion of what they owed.

"I talked with my old buddy, Palmer," Erwin said. "I told him we were only a stone's throw away from the poor house. He has a hell of an idea."

"Erwin wants to go into partnership with Palmer Brown," Levina complained to Marie a few days later.

"I absolutely will not share a house with another family. Erwin says I'll get used to it. I won't do it, Marie, I won't. I'll take in foster children, and work part-time jobs. Erwin is unreasonable. He still talks about wonderful California, as though it would be any different out west."

Marie had problems of her own with a husband who spent way too much time at the Ten Pin saloon in Chittenango, but she counted her blessings. She had a home and the means to raise her sons.

"Don't worry Vi, The Lord will provide," Marie said patting her sister's shoulder; but even as she spoke, she had serious doubts.

Erwin breezed along day by day whistling and singing seemingly without a care in the world. He figured Levina would come to her senses about the partnership, but he underestimated his determined wife. Erwin said it was the only logical way he could see to get over a rough spot. The Browns were older, their farm was paid for, and they needed help. They had a big house. It would be temporary.

Temporary or not, Levina absolutely would not consider moving in with the Browns. Undeterred, she contacted the Onondaga County Welfare office regarding foster children. After interviews, forms, and a home visit, their family increased by two girls, Coral, nine years old, and Ann, 15. Levina stretched the stipend money as far as she could. She was good at pinching pennies and cutting corners.

Penny pinching was all well and good; Levina had done that all of her life, but realistically she needed more pennies to pinch. Soon she became one of 50,000 Fashion Frock sales representatives for the Cincinnati, Ohio Company that sold over two million garments each year to budget-minded women.

Levina received loose-leaf catalog pages twice a year displaying the latest fashions for men and women along with swatches of the natural materials. Taking the catalog from house to house she measured her customers to guarantee a perfect fit. The measuring tape with the Fashion Frock label was theirs to keep. A Sunday best dress and jacket billed as sheer sophistication for slimness and chic sold for $5.98. Customers put down a deposit and paid the remainder when their orders arrived. In return Levina got out and about, felt a sense of accomplishment, and earned a commission as well as free clothing.

The Lamberts made friends in Eagle Village, enjoying evening gatherings around the kitchen table. They played Pitch, a popular card game, and the men guzzled beer; too much beer, in Levina's opinion, told bawdy jokes and laughed heartily. Phyllis fell down the stairs one night when she and Coral were eaves dropping. Tumbling all the way down the hard steps, she skinned her knees and elbows, and got to sleep with her mother and father.

Erwin hung around with his cronies on winter afternoons, going to farm equipment and cattle auctions, and playing poker at a saloon or a kitchen table. Levina felt he could make better use of his spare time.

"Ah, Ma, you worry too much," he'd say when he observed her down in the dumps demeanor.

"Someone has to worry," she said giving Erwin one of her disapproving scowls.

"Did you bring in the flannels?" Levina asked her husband curtly. Recycling was a way of life on the farm. Fresh, warm milk was strained though squares of white flannel cloth that were wedged securely under a metal stopper with openings like a colander. The large funnel-shaped strainer was used to strain milk into 10-gallon metal cans. The cans of milk were kept in the milk cooler, a large square metal box full of cold water, and trucked by the milk man to the milk factory every morning for processing.

When each milking was over, Erwin slopped a portion of milk into a battered metal cake pan for the half-wild barn cats that crawled over each other to get a drink. Taking the flannel out of the strainer before washing the utensils, he threw the milk-soaked square of cloth on the barn floor. The largest cats fought over it, each trying to grab the treasure to suck off the milk. A new flannel was used at each milking, and Levina recycled the old ones for many household uses that included home remedies.

Levina was somewhat of a homeopathic healer. When anyone in her family, or a neighbor, came down with a chest cold Levina treated them with Save the Baby poultices. The cure-all medicine that Levina swore by contained petrolatum, camphor, oregano, rosemary, and balsam oils. The lard suspension required warming before it could be poured out of the small, narrow-necked bottle. Levina warmed flannels in the kitchen stove oven, heated the bottle of Save the Baby in a pan of water, soaked hot flannels with the scalding hot aromatic liquid and slapped them on the patient's chest.

Wilda, their neighbor Harlow's live-in house keeper, walked to the Lamberts on a frigid, blustery day to ask Erwin for help with the milking. Harlow was sick in bed with a powerful chest cold. Levina drove Wilda home and gave Harlow her Save the Baby treatment.

"It will kill or cure," she said slapping a fiery hot flannel on his hairy chest. He flinched from the heat, but he got well and Levina took the credit. Phyllis can feel the hot flannel and smell the pungent medicine to this day.

The long winter finally passed, and spring crops got in the ground in good time. It was a near perfect summer. Levina kept up with most of the bills, but they didn't have a red cent to put away.

The biggest fly in the ointment for Levina, was Ann. The perky blonde simply refused to follow Levina's rules. She was sweet 16, pretty, and boy crazy. The young men were drawn to her like ants to honey. Ann was going to get into trouble; that Levina knew, and there didn't seem to be anything she could do about it. Ann would not listen to reason. The welfare worker came for the tearful teenager early on a Saturday morning.

"Good bye, little sister," Ann sobbed as she hugged Phyllis. "I love you."

"I'll write," Levina said, and she did. Ann's letter the following year was not a surprise. She was married and had a baby boy. Levina counted the months. Ann was three months pregnant when she got married.

"Didn't I say this would happen. Thank goodness the little chippy wasn't living with us." Levina sputtered to Erwin, who chuckled, saying Ann was a normal red-blooded American girl.

Levina scoffed. Ann's loose morals were the result of poor upbringing. Levina tried to make the girl see the light, but it didn't work. It would be different with her daughter. She would see to that. She never wavered from her moral rigidity.

Ann brought her husband and baby boy to see the Lamberts on a Sunday afternoon. Levina said the tow-headed little boy was as cute as a button. Erwin said he would take the little guy in a minute. The happy young mother said there was no danger of that. *Her marriage was successful. She had two more children and kept in touch for many years.*

Levina worked a couple of afternoons a week at Austin's Bakery in Chittenango. Every little bit helped. Phyllis and Erwin came into the house after chores on a brisk November day looking forward to a delicious meal. Phyllis was Daddy's helper. She loved everything about the barn, especially her daddy.

"Let's see what Ma's got to eat," he said. "She's a darn good cook." Levina was always home in time to cook supper.

Coral looked up from the kitchen table where she sat writing in a tablet. She was well behaved and very happy. Wrinkling her nose like a rabbit, she adjusted her wire rimmed glasses with one finger. Noticing Coral, little Phyllis touched her own eyes. She couldn't remember where she left her own glasses. Reading her little girl's mind as mother's often do, Levina handed Phyllis the wire rimmed specs she had left in the house. They were off her face more than they were on.

"You need to wear these so your eyes will get better. You don't want to be cross-eyed."

Phyllis liked seeing double. Coral did too.   Erwin removed the denim cap, frock, and the bib overalls   that he wore in the barn, and hung his outer clothes on wall hooks behind the kitchen coal stove. Rolling up the sleeves of his blue denim shirt, he dipped warm water out of the reservoir in the coal stove into a wash basin and washed his hands and face. He dried off briskly, patting his face with a thin towel made from a recycled cotton feed bag. The flowers on the thin fabric had faded to an indistinct pattern.

He sat down at the table, added milk and sugar to the coffee Levina poured, and picked up the newspaper. Democratic president, Franklin D. Roosevelt had defeated the Republican challenger Wendell Willkie, and would become the United States' only third-term president. A staunch Republican, any mention of the recent election irked Erwin.

"I wish they'd shut up about Roosevelt," Erwin muttered, "and be done with it."

The round oak table was set for supper of boiled potatoes, green beans, and crusty meatloaf topped with piquant homemade chili sauce. Coffee was kept warm on the back of the kitchen range where blue coal glowed blistering hot under the stove top. Levina opened the damper by turning the handle that protruded from the stovepipe. She opened one of the heavy round steel lids by fitting a metal handle with an end shaped like a claw into a groove. A blast of heat reddened her face as she added a few chunks of coal with a small shovel she kept in the black coal scuttle. The fire blazed with the distinct odor of coal gas although the open damper allowed most of the smoke and fumes to escape outdoors.

"Good vittles, Ma." Erwin stirred cream and sugar into the coffee in a whirlpool the way he always did, causing a tiny wave to overflow onto the saucer. Taking a slow sip of the sweet liquid, he poured coffee from the saucer back into his cup and leaned back in his chair. It was his ritual, and it never varied. Bowser shook his head, making his ears flap like wings, scratched behind one ear, settled down on the linoleum next to Erwin's chair and rolled over on his back. Erwin reached down to scratch the dog's soft, furry belly. One of Bowser's hind legs pumped in unison with the petting like someone pedaling a bicycle with one foot. Levina walked past Erwin's chair, and he moved his hand in a gesture to pat his wife's bottom. She side stepped quickly.

"What's the matter, Ma? Can't I get a little feel?" Erwin chuckled.

Four – 1940-1942

The Lamberts at Eagle Village

By 1940 most of Western Europe, except for Great Britain, was controlled by Germany and Italy. President Roosevelt admired England's stand off against Adolph Hitler. He and Prime Minister Winston Churchill were in cahoots, and the United States was retooling for military production. U. S. military rearmament produced factory jobs. The Great Depression was coming to an end. A factory worker could earn up to $1,250 per year. Levina's brother, Marinus, earned good money at Precision Castings, a tool shop in Manlius. Marinus called his work place "The Precision." Levina wished Erwin would consider a factory job, but, he said that wasn't his style.

"Palmer was here today," Erwin announced at supper time. "He says his missus is failing; they really need help."

"I thought we put that berserk idea behind us," Levina retorted. "So what does it have to do with us?"

"Nothing," Erwin said sitting down with the newspaper. "Nothing at all."

Erwin was running out of patience. He worked like a dog, and still they couldn't get a single penny ahead toward a place of their own. He could not understand why sharing a house with the Browns was such a problem. Their children were grown and gone. It was a big house. He was determined to go into partnership, but he wasn't sure, just yet, how to convince his wife.

The seasons of Phyllis's childhood tumbled along like somersaults, and before anyone could say "Jack Robinson," it was her fifth birthday.

"Time flies. I can't believe Phyllis is five years old already," Levina said with a deep sigh. "She's not a baby anymore." Then, with the snap of a finger, April was over.

Erwin was concentrating on spring work in Eagle Village when Hitler's mighty military machine invaded Holland on May 10, 1940. The German tactic called blitzkrieg, "lightning war," was based on speed and surprise. Rotterdam was severely damaged by German bombs and Hitler threatened Amsterdam would be next. The overwhelmed Dutch army surrendered after six days of fighting. Levina was frantic when the news reached

America. She could not imagine German troops goose-stepping through her beloved Holland. She prayed for her Dutch relatives and hoped every day for a reply to her letters. When the rare letter got through, it was heavily censored. Only the good Lord knew what was really happening.

Phyllis was "mommy's helper" when Levina went on the road showing the Fashion Frocks catalog to neighbors. The women enjoyed having company and getting caught up on gossip while browsing pictures of the latest fashions. Best of all, they usually made a purchase.

Levina stopped regularly to see Mrs. Henderson, because, "the poor thing," as Levina called her, could not get to stores. Something was wrong with Mrs. Henderson's legs. Mr. Henderson lifted his wife from the car to her wheelchair when they came to visit. Phyllis thought it was lucky that she was a small woman. She sat in her wheelchair with a crocheted shawl covering her legs when Levina and Phyllis walked into the house.

Phyllis couldn't sit still. Levina suggested she "run along and play." The little girl scampered outside, kicking the dusty driveway with the toes of her shoes. A white mother hen and chicks scurried around the yard, scratching here and there with stiff legs and knees that seemed backward.

"There's nothing cuter than baby chicks," Phyllis said aloud, mimicking her mother. She picked up one of the yellow balls of fluff without the hen noticing and ran to the house with the tiny chick cupped delicately in her small hands. Frail Mrs. Henderson sat in her wheelchair flipping through the clothes catalog as Levina urged her to look at this page and that.

Phyllis opened her hands to show off the chick and, just as quickly, the little bird squirmed out of her hands and dropped into Mrs. Henderson's lap wildly flapping its tiny wings. Mrs. Henderson screamed and shooed the bird with frantic arm thrusts, trying to rid herself of the squirming thing.

"Get it off me!" she yelled. "Get it off! Get it off!"

The little girl was startled and confused. How could a grown woman, even if she was in a wheelchair, be afraid of a tiny chick? In a dither, she grabbed the poor chick off the floor where it had fallen, and ran for the door, with Mrs. Henderson's frantic screams following her into the yard. That was the day Phyllis learned about phobias.

Phyllis and Coral counted days on the big Currier and Ives calendar that hung on the kitchen wall, crossing out each day until it was Friday, June 27, the last day of school. Little sisters and brothers were invited to attend the end-of-school program called "Exercises."

The excited girls skipped down the main road that morning past sturdy maple trees on the way to the small, white school house. The building had one room with windows lining each side, big blackboards on the front wall and a coal stove in the back. The teacher's desk was in front of the black board and students' desks were lined up in rows facing the teacher.

Syncopated chimes from the school bell echoed across the fields as the girls walked. Coral grabbed Phyllis's hand and picked up the pace when she heard boys' taunting voices from behind. The same two boys who mocked her every day for wearing glasses circled the girls threateningly, dancing around them chanting: "Four eyes. Four eyes."

The tallest kid pulled the skin down around his eyes with his fingers exposing bloodshot whites and stretching his mouth into a grotesque, ghoulish expression. The other boy growled and poked at the girls. Phyllis screamed, closing her eyes and clutching Coral's arm. As quickly as the boys had arrived, they grew bored with their prank and ran ahead down the road pushing at each other.

"I'm telling!" Coral yelled after them, "I'm telling!"

At noon mothers lugged baskets of food to school. Fathers left their fields behind to enthusiastically applaud the performing students who had rehearsed songs and pieces for weeks. Everything was memorized. Prizes were awarded for attendance, deportment and scholarship. The next day summer vacation began.

Suburban Park was the most exciting place that Phyllis could imagine, and it was just a short ride down the road from their farm. Old timers said the amusement park had been going strong since the late 1800's. It was the place to be on balmy summer evenings when families and friends gathered in the picnic grove with enough food to feed threshers. Each woman brought a favorite dish to pass; Levina's specialty was baked beans. Erwin and his cronies swigged beer out of stubby brown bottles, smoked cigars, talked in hushed tones from time to time and broke out into raucous laughter that mystified the children.

Phyllis and her friends were on pins and needles according to their mothers, waiting for their parents to finish eating so they could go on rides. The clickety-clack, clickety-clack of the Comet roller coaster echoed across the small park as it labored up the first steep incline clinging to the track on a rickety wood frame. Reaching the summit, the Comet jerked, then picked up speed plummeting downward to the blood curdling screams of excited riders. Cars tilted sideways around curves, certain to jump the track, then glided back to the gate. Some of the screamers rode again and again.

Phyllis and Coral ran to catch the little train pulled by a steam locomotive barely big enough to hold the rotund engineer. Scrambling into one of the small open-air cars they took a seat and waved at Levina who stood watching with other mothers. The smiling engineer wearing a gray-and-white-striped denim engineer's cap and bib overalls, shoveled coal into the fire box that belched sulfurous fumes.

"All aboard!"

The wheels of the train groaned to life just as the roller coaster zoomed overhead with a terrible clatter. The tracks crisscrossed directly under the Comet's wooden framework that wobbled and shook in a windstorm of its own making. The girls ducked as the speeding Comet with screaming passengers zoomed down the first incline. Paying no attention to the roller coaster, the engineer pulled a rope attached to a whistle as the train passed a small white building with an outdoor stage where trick dogs performed. The train chugged through the magical woods of whispering trees, and back to the station near the Comet's entrance where diehard devotees waited for another death-defying ride.

Scampering off the train, Phyllis and Coral ran lickety-split to the merry-go-round where brightly painted wooden horses slid up and down greasy metal poles in time to calliope music. Kids clamored to secure a favorite pony grasping the reins as they twirled around and around. Mothers and fathers stood on the dusty path waving to their smiling children as if they didn't have a worry in the world. Thoughts of war had been packed away for the night.

After the rides, Phyllis and Coral skipped along dusty trails, staring at monkeys and parrots crammed into small cages. They eyed the colorful birds who simply winked.

"Polly want a cracker?" The parrots refused to talk, although the girls knew they could if they wanted to. Small monkeys scoured each other's fur examining and munching whatever treats they found. Roller skaters waltzed to music in an open-air pavilion near the arcade.

50

Phyllis was happy beyond description roaming around the most exciting place in her small world. Colored lights on rides dipped and rose against a darkening sky. Excited voices mingled, and sparks flew from the ceiling above multi-colored bumper cars in crash after fun-filled crash. Coral wandered off with a friend her own age.

Carousel music wafted through the dusty air as Phyllis skipped toward the bench where her mother said she would wait. Her mother wasn't there and she was startled to hear something that made her feel sick in the pit of her stomach. She ran toward the sound of her mother's voice pleading, "No, no, no."

"Aw come on," someone urged, "what cha got to lose?"

Friends were daring her mother, pushing her toward the bomber ride. To the little girl's horror, her mother climbed into the capsule with their handsome neighbor, Harlow. She didn't hear Phyllis crying "no mommy, no mommy." A mean looking man slammed and locked the door with a steel bar as Phyllis held her hand to her mouth in disbelief. Phyllis and Levina had watched that awful ride soar and dive many times. Now her mother was trapped in it as her dad stood calmly by swigging a beer, and talking with other men.

Two cylindrical capsules teetered and rotated precariously on either end of a central steel bar as the bomber took off. The monstrous machine roared into the evening sky gyrating and plummeting repeatedly toward the ground on grating gears. Each time it lunged, Phyllis echoed her mother's sickening screams.

Phyllis prayed through clenched teeth, and when Levina escaped the bomber ride, she knew it was because she had promised God that if He protected her mother, she would never go on that ride. She never did.

As the sky darkened, families sat on blankets spread

over a grassy hillside watching fireworks explode in colorful eruptions across the evening sky. The crowd hooted and hollered, inspired by the spectacle, a temporary escape from a troubled world that was teetering on the brink of World War II.

On August 14 President Roosevelt and England's Prime Minister Winston Churchill met in secret aboard a ship anchored at Placentia Bay off Newfoundland where the Atlantic Charter was signed. The United States government aided the European war effort with weapons and supplies funneled by ship across the north Atlantic to Great Britain under President Roosevelt's Lend-Lease Program. The name of the plan was a misnomer. The American government was neither lending nor leasing—it was instead helping to fund the terrible war that Nazi Germany had started. Most Americans were isolationists and fervently opposed involvement in another European war.

Summer was peaceful on the little farm in Eagle Village. Life was good and Phyllis had no reason to think life should be any other way. She sat on her father's hay wagon under a sunny summer sky with neighborhood twins, Joyce and Janet, and their younger brother, Teddy, who was Phyllis's age. Erwin sang "Oh My Darlin' Clementine," while he picked up hay scatterings with his pitch fork that had been left behind by the hay loader. Erwin did not waste anything. He repeatedly twirled the hay around his pitchfork into tidy bundles and tossed the bundles on the wagon. It was like a dance the way he moved, twirled and tossed. He would clear up the immediate area, jump on the wagon, and flick the reins to move the horses ahead, tie the reins to the hay rack and jump back to the ground, whistling while he worked

The kids chatted and giggled the way little kids do. Phyllis was excited because their nice neighbor, Harlow, had promised her a calf ride later.

Reaching up every time a bundle was tossed their way, they scattered the hay in an explosion of stalks, leaves, and dust. Tiny bullet-shaped insects landed on the wagon and on the children, who touched their tiny pointed ends making the insects jump.

Sliding her little hand under a new bundle of hay on the wagon, Phyllis twirled her fingers the way her father twirled his pitch fork, brushing tiny leaves that clung to alfalfa stems. The idyllic day, like something out of a Robert Louis Stevenson poem, was suddenly shattered by Phyllis's screams. The little girl screamed in pain as tears rolled down her cheeks, screamed as she yanked her hand from under the hay and saw a small, gray field mouse clamped securely to one of her fingers with razor sharp teeth. Blood streamed down her hand. Hysterical, she screamed louder, shaking her hand violently. The mouse held on. Blood streamed down her arm. Joyce, Janet and Teddy stared at the mouse, adding their voices to the screaming melee. Phyllis jumped to her feet.

"Daddy! Daddy!" she yelled frantically.

Bowser spun around in a circle, barking sharply, looking toward Phyllis and then at Erwin.

"What the Hell!" Erwin jumped onto the wagon in

one fluid motion, grabbing his panic-stricken daughter and somehow ejecting the mouse that he crushed beneath one heavy work shoe. Hearing the commotion, Levina dropped her clothes basket under the clothes line and ran to the nearby hay field to comfort her distraught little girl.

"Oh dear lord, oh dear lord," Levina chanted as she carried her sobbing, bleeding daughter to the safety of the farmhouse kitchen. The mouse attack was a tale oft told stretching over the next 20 years.

Ray Hale, a bachelor neighbor who lived with his parents on a big farm on Hale Road, roared into the Lambert's driveway in the early afternoon of Sunday, December 7, 1941, screeched to a halt and jumped out of his truck.

"We've been attacked. The Japs bombed our ships at Pearl Harbor!" he yelled as he burst into the house. He had heard the news on the radio.

The Japanese had launched a sneak air raid on the United States Pacific fleet at Pearl Harbor, Hawaii. The next day the Lamberts and their neighbors sat around the radio in the Hale kitchen listening to President Franklin D. Roosevelt deliver a seven-minute speech to a Joint Session of Congress. The speech began:

"Yesterday, December 7, 1941—a date which will live in infamy—the United States of America was suddenly and deliberately attacked by naval and air forces of the Empire of Japan."

Within an hour of the speech, Congress passed a formal declaration of war against Japan. The deadly attack pushed public opinion from isolationism to patriotism.

On December 11, Italian dictator, Benito Mussolini, and shortly afterwards, Germany's Adolf Hitler, in two separate announcements, declared war on the United States, hurtling the United States of America into the European conflict.

The grownups talked and fretted about the war while kids played war games. Their parents told them not to worry, and they didn't.

"We need to get a radio Ma," Erwin said soon after the war began. "To keep up with the news."

"We can't afford a radio Erwin," Levina said emphatically.

Erwin didn't often override his wife's wishes, but he was convinced that they needed a radio and he bought one at Tyler's combination furniture store and funeral parlor in Chittenango without another word. By then 80 percent of the U. S. population owned radio sets. Levina said Erwin spent money like a drunken sailor which, of course, was not true. He rarely spent money. Despite her opposition to the purchase, Levina enjoyed the pleasant diversion of radio programs, especially, soap opera drama that dominated the daytime airwaves. Little Phyllis's romantic personality was undoubtedly programmed listening to love story after unrequited love story. Where was "happily ever after?"

Phyllis and her mother came home from visiting Aunt Marie on a rainy spring afternoon to find Levina's ordinarily spotless kitchen in disarray. The table was littered with beer bottles and playing cards, and a cat had pooped under the table.

"My word, Erwin!" Levina exclaimed, although Erwin was nowhere to be seen.

Levina was in the back room getting a mop pail and rags to clean up the mess when someone knocked sharply on the outside door. Without saying a word, Levina took Phyllis quietly by the hand and crawled under the bed in the downstairs bedroom.

"Why are we under the bed mommy?"

"Shh," Levina said putting her fingers to her lips. "It's probably that pesky Fuller Brush salesman. I don't need anything."

The knocking soon stopped and they crawled out to finish cleaning.

"The pesky brush man came to the door today," Phyllis reported at supper. "We hid under the bed."

Levina, who was still upset about the mess Erwin and his cronies had left in the kitchen, didn't say a word, but she felt her face flush.

"Brush man? I expect it was a bill collector," Erwin said with a chuckle.

"Erwin, that is not funny," Levina retorted.

"No it isn't, but you can't see the woods for the trees. We are getting nowhere fast; we've gotta cut expenses. Palmer and his missus need the help and we need the money. None of us are getting any younger."

Levina got up from the table and began briskly clearing away dishes.

"It's time for bed girls," she said to Coral and Phyllis. "Up the golden stairs."

Five – 1942-1944

Phyllis had no inkling on an ordinary spring day in 1942 that her life was about to change drastically. Coral went to school as usual. Levina had errands to do and she took her daughter to spend the day at Austin's Bakery Shop. Phyllis never went back to the Eagle Village farm.

Going to the bakery was better than a party. The basement area, where the ovens were located, smelled wonderful. Earl took bread out of the oven, and Phyllis inhaled the aroma. After the bread cooled, he ran it through the slicer and wrapped it in wax paper sealing the ends with a hot iron. Phyllis liked the aroma of fresh bread and the smell of hot wax.

"You're a good little helper," Earl said as she happily frosted her favorite half-moon cookies, half chocolate and half vanilla. Earl put the cookies she frosted in a white box saying she could take them home. Reaching up to a large spool of string that hung from the ceiling, he tied white string around the box.

"Daddy will be happy," she told Earl, "he really   likes cookies."

Sitting on the front stoop waiting for pretend big sister, Barbara to come home from school, she watched the ice man arrive in his old truck that was dripping water from thawing blocks of ice. He grabbed huge blocks with big tongs and carried the ice on his shoulders to fill two iceboxes. He tweaked Phyllis's nose when he walked past on the way back to his truck.

"What's in the box?"

"Cookies for my Daddy."

Earl, Edith and their daughter Barbara, who was "big sister" to Phyllis, lived upstairs over the shop. On holidays Phyllis and the family watched parades from the second floor balcony that overlooked Genesee Street. When Barbra got home they played board games until supper time. Aunt Edith served spaghetti because Phyllis loved it best.

After supper Levina's friends, Julia and Art, arrived with Levina in their car to pick up Phyllis at the bakery. Coral was sitting in the back seat.

"What 'cha got in the box?" Coral asked.

"Cookies for Daddy."

Art drove out of the village up Brinkerhoff Hill toward home. Phyllis couldn't stop thinking about giving the cookies to her Daddy. Art stopped the car half way up the hill at a big house that was located next door to his brother, Perry's house. Bowser was sitting on the porch steps. Phyllis petted his head asking him what he was doing there.

No one had lived in the house since Ma and Pa Button died. They went inside and a funny thing happened. Levina made coffee as though she was at her own house. The old folk's olden furniture was still there. The house smelled like dust and moth balls.

"Where's Daddy?" Phyllis asked.

"He's busy on the farm," Levina said.

"But I have cookies for him," Phyllis pouted. "I need to see him."

"Not now."

"Why?" Phyllis asked, "I have to."

"No more, ifs, ands, or buts young lady. We'll be staying here for a while. It's almost your bed time."

Levina fixed hot cocoa for the girls, and after they drank it, she took them upstairs to the bedroom. Phyllis's skinny, brown Teddy Bear was waiting on the bed. (*She still has the love-worn toy*).

Coral cried the next day when Levina said she would have to move in with another family. Coral's welfare worker was in Onondaga County, and they had moved to Madison County. She said Coral should act like a big girl and not cry Coral didn't feel like a big girl. Levina promised to write letters, and she kept her word. *On June 16, 1951, Phyllis was a bridesmaid in Coral's wedding.*

Levina puttered and fussed cleaning and cooking but she did not do any explaining. The little girl missed her Daddy and Coral and life the way it had been. Wandering outside with Bowser, the dog sniffed his way into the dark, dusty carriage house in the back yard his tail wagging with the excitement of exploration. The barn was packed with junk: old tires and boxes, chicken crates, horse harnesses, and a buggy with a broken wheel. Poking around Phyllis noticed a big, brown eye peeking out from under an accumulation of odds and ends covered with a tattered piece of canvas. Pulling off the tarp she found the biggest rocking horse she could imagine.

"Poor thing," she said, "you don't look comfortable."

Bowser barked in short, staccato yips the way dogs do when they are excited. Phyllis tossed junk out of the way releasing the hobby horse.

"Who left you out here all alone," she asked, petting his black wooden nose.

Dragging him to the wide doorway, she mounted her steed, rocking and rocking as hard as she could until he bucked right out of the building into the driveway. "Yippee-ki-yay," she yelled as Bowser nipped at the wooden heels. She wished it was a real pony, but since it wasn't, imagining would have to do. Imagining always made her feel better.

Phyllis spent her days at Austin's Bakery helping Earl and getting to lick sweet batter out of mixing bowls while her mother looked for a job. Earl baked and Edith waited on customers. Levina seemed happy the day she came back to the shop saying she would be keeping books at Ezra Cook's grist mill.

When Levina went to the mill to work, Phyllis went along. She would start first grade that fall. She played with mill cats and explored endless, dusty chambers. That was until she caught the mumps.

A neighbor girl, who was staying with her, was painting Phyllis's fingernails the afternoon she heard the chugging sound of a tractor engine. Pressing her face against the living room window that overlooked Brinkerhoff Hill road, she saw her father riding on the top of a tall, rounded load of hay. The farm where they had lived was on the same road as the Button house, but it was the first time she had seen her daddy since they moved. She wanted to run out and grab him, but her legs wouldn't move. Tears ran down her face as she watched the wagon with her father disappear around a curve in the road.

Levina and Phyllis did a lot of walking that summer when Levina worked at the feed mill in Chittenango and they lived in the Button House on Brinkerhoff Hill. Rain or shine every weekday morning they walked down the hill that Levina called "the long mile," and trudged back up every afternoon. Occasionally a friend stopped to give them a ride, but mostly, according to Levina, they relied on Shanks Mare.

"Is this a mountain?" Phyllis asked when they were walking home on a particularly hot afternoon.

"No, it just seems like one because we're tired.

"My word!" Levina exclaimed, cupping her face in her hands as a jalopy roared past stirring up dust. "That was too close for comfort." She was tired of walking every day.

Russell Austin, Earl's brother, stood outside his dairy barn door most afternoons watching for them. He liked talking with Levina.

"It's a bad year for mosquitoes," Russell said fiercely rubbing one hairy arm. "I just scratch the bites until they bleed; that stops the itching."

Levina paused, but Phyllis kept walking. It was hot and she wanted to get home.

"Phyllis! Wait! Wait for me."

The little girl stopped by the side of the road pushing pebbles around with the toe of her shoe.

"Them god-dammed Kraut U-boats are doing a number on our ships in the Atlantic," Russell noted, still scratching his arms.

"Yes, it is very sad." Levina wished he would not cuss in front of her daughter.

"The Brits held the Krauts and the Wops at El Alamein though," he said, chortling and scratching at the same time.

"It's awfully hot," Levina said. "But we won't have to take this walk much longer. Mr. Baton is renting me a place in town. I just found out today."

"Well then, I guess I won't see you," Russell said. "That's too bad." He liked Levina.

Levina and Phyllis did their banking at The State Bank of Chittenango where Levina had her checking account and Phyllis kept her meager savings. Levina usually chatted with the bank president, Henry Baton, who she secretly called "The Big Cheese."

"Hi, Levina," he said when they walked into the bank earlier that Friday afternoon. Levina was pleased that he called her by her first name.

"Your Ma's a terrific cook," he said winking at Phyllis. "We go way back," he noted, referring to when Levina worked at Howard's Restaurant across the street from the bank. "Too bad Florence sold the restaurant," he said.

"Yes," Levina said, "too bad for a lot of people. I'm not looking forward to the walk up Brinkerhoff; it's just too hot. I pray every night I can find a place I can afford in the village."

"The other side of my mother's house is empty. I'll rent it to you reasonable," the Big Cheese said, insinuating it might not be quite as reasonable if it were anyone else. Levina and Phyllis were soon village residents.

Phyllis met her first best friend, red haired, freckle-faced Hazel, on the August day when they moved into the Baton House. Hazel fidgeted, standing in her front lawn watching Phyllis and Bowser in their back yard. A vacant lot separated them. Phyllis didn't dare say hello, but Hazel did. The two six-year-olds soon wore a dirt path through the field running back and forth to each other's houses, and when September arrived they started school together. Having a best friend was the best thing in the world.

Almost a year had passed since Ray Hale had come to the farm to tell the Lamberts about the Japanese attack on Pearl Harbor. Levina said it seemed like they had been at war forever. Back then Phyllis didn't understand what was happening. Now she was in first grade, felt a whole lot older and knew lots of things about the war. Americans hated the German dictator, Adolph Hitler,

Italy's prime minister, Benito Mussolini, and the Japanese Prime Minister, Hideki Tojo. Japan's Emperor Hirohito was also a despised household name.

Everything with a *"Made in Japan"* trademark was trashed. On the margins of school papers kids drew Nazi swastikas, the Japanese bright red "rising sun," and Kilroy, the American graffiti character with the big nose. They lived with blackouts, talk of the mysterious black market, rationing, shortages, and air raid drills.

"We're going to the show tonight," Phyllis told Hazel as they walked home from school on a Friday afternoon. Now and then Phyllis went directly home from school rather than meeting her mother at Ezra Cook's mill. Their landlady, Mrs. Baton, who lived in the other side of the house, would be there if Phyllis needed anything. Bowser waited by the back steps wagging his tail.

"See you later," she said to Hazel who continued across the field to her house. "Good doggie," she said patting Bowser's head before they went into the house.

Levina and Phyllis walked the short distance to the movie theater in the center of the village that night bundled up for winter walking. A double-feature was playing, so they got to see two movies one after the other. Movie Tone News brought the war into the theatre with black and white news reels from various fighting fronts described with patriotic fervor.

"Allies fight back," boomed the commentator's deep voice, as the newsreel projected a picture of General Dwight Eisenhower on the screen. By November, 1942, the United States was fighting back in North Africa.

Hollywood capitalized on the news of the day, churning out war movies in rapid succession. Phyllis had nightmares after seeing a horrific movie about the African theatre, where enemy tanks chased down allied soldiers hiding in fox holes dug in the sand. She had no idea why they called the war a theatre. As if the tanks weren't

63

scary enough, the second feature zombie movie gave Phyllis night horrors. Zombies rose up out of coffins walking stiff-legged through the city chasing good people. That night, after she was asleep, the zombies stumbled into Phyllis's bedroom.

Aunt Marie invited Levina and Phyllis to Christmas dinner at the farm. Phyllis brought along her new Princess doll. She had long blonde curls, and wore a beautiful, light blue gown trimmed with lace. Phyllis thought she was the prettiest doll in the whole wide world.

"Did Santa bring you the pretty doll?" Aunt Marie asked.

"No," she said, "it's from my Daddy. We found it on the porch."

As far as Phyllis knew, her mother and father were mad at each other. Otherwise, why weren't they still living together? Phyllis didn't know if she would ever see her Daddy again.

By 1943, government-issued ration coupons were needed to purchase many different items. Just about everything was scarce. Kids saved aluminum foil they peeled off gum and candy wrappers, molding the metal foil into large balls that were donated to the cause. They bought victory stamps in school and picked up metal cans that were flattened and recycled. Customers were required to turn in an empty toothpaste tube before buying a new one. Just about everybody planted a victory garden.

Levina borrowed a car from a mill worker during her lunch hour on a day in mid-March, because she was having a Stanley Party that night and needed to pick up refreshment items from the grocery store. In a hurry and thinking about things other than driving, she didn't see a pick-up truck as she turned into her driveway. The driver swerved to avoid Levina's car grazing the tree in front of the house.

"Why the hell don't you look where you're going, lady," the truck driver yelled as he jumped out to inspect the damage. The truck fender was dented but the tree looked okay. A tarp was strapped over the bed of the truck, and the driver adjusted the ropes.

"Oh, I'm sorry, I'm sorry," Levina said getting out of the car. "It isn't my car."

The irate man mumbled obscenities under his breath, jumped back in the truck, gunned the motor and drove down the street.

Levina was still upset about the accident as she sat at the kitchen table that evening counting stamps in her rationing book before her guests arrived. She used stamps earlier that day when she bought coffee and sugar for the party.

Levina's friends arrived at seven o'clock light hearted and happy to have an evening out. Phyllis helped her mother take the coats. The demonstrator promoted Stanley products, and guests replenished their supplies of household cleaning items, spices, patent medicines, etc. If you needed it—Stanley had it. Levina earned points toward free products, and everyone had a good time.

"I had a frightening experience today," Levina said talking about the rude man who was driving a suspicious truck. "I suspect," she said, pouring more tea, " he was dealing in the Black Market. He was in a big hurry, and seemed nervous. The back of the truck was covered with canvas. I expect he was peddling cigarettes and whiskey."

Phyllis walked a quarter of a mile down a steep hill from the school to Ezra Cook's feed mill and into the cluttered, dusty office where her mother worked.

"Hi, Phippy, don't forget to change your clothes before you feed the cats."

Ezra, who owned the mill, said the cats were good little hunters who deserved a slug of milk every day. It was Phyllis's job, he said, "to feed the cats who hunted the rats that infested the mill."

A quart of milk in a glass bottle with a cardboard cap was waiting by the door every afternoon. She opened the bottle and poured milk into a large, battered metal pan as cats of every size and color jostled for position. Yowling and jumping, they twined around each other like cooked spaghetti, sometimes scratching Phyllis's legs in their excitement. Milk usually got poured on feline heads but others licked it off. The cats licked the inside of the pan clean with their tongues, but the outside was coated with gooey, yellow dried milk and dirt.

Roaming around the dusty, three-story wood frame building usually put Phyllis (who the workmen called young lady) in minor jeopardy. If she didn't skin a knee, or an elbow, she got slivers from the wood slides. Levina kept a bottle of mercurochrome, a needle, a book of matches, a roll of gauze, and adhesive tape in her desk drawer to dress her daughter's frequent wounds. The red colored antiseptic did not sting the way brown iodine did and it was a pretty color. Levina drew little faces on Phyllis's skin with the glass stopper that was attached to the mercurochrome bottle cap.

A sewing needle was stuck in a bar of soap ready for sliver removal. Just thinking about the process made Phyllis cringe as her mother swabbed the area with mercurochrome. Levina held the needle in the flame of a match for sterilization, and began the surgery. She manipulated the needle deep enough to get under the offending piece of wood so it could be lifted out. As Phyllis grew older, she removed slivers by herself.

It wasn't that Phyllis was accident prone, the problem was having EB. Her friends fell down just as often as she did, but they didn't get hurt. When she fell it resulted in bruises, blisters and sores. If her ankle got kicked, it broke the skin. If she hit her elbow or a knuckle against something, the skin broke or blistered. Every mishap resulted in physical injury. Blisters and broken skin on knees, elbows, knuckles, shins, and ankles were the norm. When she turned over in bed, rubbing the skin raw on an elbow, she thought about Grandma Van Dyke who Levina said had the same problem. She was rarely without a bandage on some part of her skinny, scarred body. Her mother asked her not to dig off the scabs, but she did it anyway.

Oats and wheat from large grain silos were ground and mixed with molasses into fragrant cow feed called grist. The stone grinder shuttered, groaned and chugged as workers filled 100-pound burlap bags with grist and tied each bag with twine. Dust motes danced in the air and dusty cob webs hung from rough sawn beams like ragged lace curtains. Plump bags of grain were given a shove to start them downward along wide board slides, formed with raised edges to hold the speeding bags in place as they careened from floor to floor. Phyllis glided down the slides sitting on empty burlap bags.

Phyllis enjoyed playing alone in the mill. Capturing black, hard-shelled beetles that she found in ground cow feed, she bivouacked her "soldiers" in their own feed-filled cigar box. The cylindrical bugs with hairy legs burrowed in the feed like miniature army tanks. "Vroom, vroom." She mimicked the sounds she heard her cousins Kenny and Jerry use when they played with their toy trucks on Aunt Marie and Uncle Fred's farm. It was easy pretending she was somebody else living someone else's life. It became a habit.

Birthday and Christmas gifts from Phyllis's father appeared on Mrs. Baton's enclosed front porch, but he didn't come in to see his daughter. Phyllis had only seen her father twice in a year and a half. The first time was when he was riding on top of the load of hay the summer before she started school. The second time he saw her first.

"Hey you two! Stop that!" Erwin yelled.

Phyllis and Hazel, partners in crime, stood throwing stones through broken windows of a small, vacant building near the corner of Falls Boulevard and Perryville Road, when they heard a man yell. It took a few seconds before Phyllis realized it was her father. The girls dropped their stones, bolted like scared rabbits and ran in the opposite direction.

"Come back, Babe," her father yelled, "I was just teasing."

Phyllis only knew they had been caught red-handed. What if her mother found out? They ran all the way home.

Ray Hale, a bachelor neighbor from Eagle Village, was sitting with Levina at the kitchen table when the girls got home. He was a regular caller. Phyllis didn't like him hanging around. Ray had a large face with red cheeks and a shiny receding forehead. He wore a fedora and grinned all the time. He kidded around and tried to tickle Phyllis, who hated to be tickled.

When Ray and her mother sat on the couch, Phyllis crawled along the top of the backrest making rude noises. Levina threatened to spank her every time, and every time Phyllis ran to the bathroom locking the door. She stayed inside until her mother calmed down; wishing her father would come to visit.

World War II raged on across six continents during the spring of '43, but life in Chittenango, New York was predictable. American factories were mobilized by the federal government to produce weapons of war. Detroit manufactured Sherman tanks instead of automobiles.

There were blackouts at night, when everyone pulled their shades and street lights were turned off so the enemy could not see their town. Phyllis imagined war planes flying overhead the way she saw them in movies. Old men acting as air raid wardens walked around town making sure no lights could be seen. If you got a knock on your door, you knew your dark green shades needed to be adjusted.

Phyllis and Hazel darted around in the dark with quart canning jars capturing lightning bugs. The lights on their little tails flashed off and on like the beer signs in the Genesee Saloon next door had done before blackouts.

"Hey," Phyllis said, "don't these bugs know there's a blackout." They brought their bottles of bugs into the house to show Levina, who said they should let the poor things go. They said they would, but not until after they showed Hazel's mother and father, and off they went. Bowser bounced along behind them. Half way across the field Phyllis stopped walking, rummaged in her pocket and came up with a pack of candy cigarettes.

"Want one?" The two "smoked" the slim, white cigarettes with affection (just like in the movies) as they rushed on to Hazel's house with the imprisoned lightning bugs. When the sweet, hard candy dissolved on their tongues to butt size they ate the rest.

Mrs. Baton stayed with Phyllis when Ray took Levina to a carnival of some sort on a balmy spring evening.

"Mr. Hale seems like a nice man," Mrs. Baton said as she and Phyllis played a game of checkers.

"I don't like him," Phyllis countered with a pout. She had made up her mind and that was it.

"I brought you a nice present," Levina said the next morning at breakfast. "If you're a good girl today, you can have it after school."

Levina was disappointed that Phyllis had received an "unsatisfactory," for deportment on her report card. Every day was a test of her behavior.

There was no doubt that Phyllis and Hazel were little devils. Some people even called them brats. Levina said it was misplaced exuberance. They got picked on by mean classmates, and older students were assigned as body guards when they were on the playground. The guards worked well, and having the attention of big kids made Phyllis and Hazel feel important.

As she talked, Levina ripped open a small envelope of Mother Gray's Sweet Powders and mixed the whitish-gray powder with water on a table spoon. Phyllis cringed. Levina seemed to think she might have worms because she had been scratching her bottom. The non-prescription medicine used as a diuretic and purgative was pretty much guaranteed to heal whatever ailed you, or so people said. The laxatives were Calomel (mercurous chloride) and mandrake. The non-laxative ingredients were licorice, slippery elm, bicarbonate of soda, anise, and sugar. It tasted like poison but the powders had to go down. If that wasn't bad enough, she had to take a spoonful of cod liver oil every morning. It smelled like the foulest of dead fish, and it made the little girl gag, but Levina said fish oil was good for her.

Lilies of the Valley bloomed at the roots of a craggy old tree in an abandoned cemetery across the street from the school. Phyllis noticed the flowers from the sidewalk, and she climbed over the low stone wall to pick a bouquet for her mother. Sitting on a tombstone she watched the branches of really tall trees bending and bowing. After

70

considerable thought, she had come to the conclusion that trees made the wind. She could see it as plain as the nose on her face. The branches only moved when the wind was blowing and that was enough proof for her.

Walking into the cluttered mill office where her mother kept the books, she presented the flowers knowing her mother loved the tiny, bell-shaped blossoms.

"They're my favorite kind," she said, gently holding the fragrant flowers to her nose. Lily of the Valley was also her mother's favorite cologne.

"Watch the door," Levina said after she put the flowers in a glass of water. "I've got to tinkle."

Levina used a glass canning jar she kept under the desk to pee. She told Aunt Marie she could not tolerate using the mill out house because of the pestilential stench. Phyllis didn't understand the big words, but she knew it meant the outhouse stunk to high heaven, and she held her nose whenever she went inside. Old catalogs and magazines were piled between the two holes in the wooden seat where pee and poop dropped into a dark, smelly pit. Pages from the catalogs and magazines were used for wiping, but they didn't work very well. There wasn't any toilet paper.

"Phyllis, were you a good girl today?" Of course she gave a good report. She was anxious to see the present Levina had mentioned at breakfast. That was partly why she picked the flowers.

After feeding the cats, she hurried home ahead of her mother. Bowser was waiting on the back stoop, wagging his tail for dear life. He followed Phyllis into the house where she found a toy clown with a pink and lavender cloth body and a smiling celluloid face propped up on the kitchen table. Phyllis had been hoping for a kaleidoscope.

She didn't like the clown, and she threw it against the wall denting both of its rosy celluloid cheeks. By the time she realized what she had done it was too late. All of a

sudden she was not mad anymore; she felt sad seeing him
lying there like a wounded soldier. Picking up the toy,
she sat on the floor crying at the top of her lungs as
though her heart was broken.

Hearing Phyllis's screams, Mrs. Baton hurried over
from her side of the house. "Whatever is the matter? Did
you hurt yourself again?"

Phyllis held up the clown, saying its face was broken
but not volunteering any details. She had to think of an
explanation before her mother got home.

"Did you drop him?" Mrs. Baton asked?

"Uh huh," Phyllis said cuddling the poor little thing.

It was Phyllis's second summer at the mill and the
workers thought of her as one of the crew. She loved
being the center of attention. She was especially cajoled
to join the cats in rodent extermination.

"Get the little bastards," the men chided in raspy
voices through tobacco stained teeth as she wandered
around the mill. "Just pretend they're Japs."

Mice ate grain. Grain was needed to feed the troops.
According to seven-year-old-rationale, the mice had to
go. Climbing up open wooden stairways to the top floor
where oats and wheat were stored in large bins, she
waded, knee deep through shifting piles of grain
searching for baby mice. Her mission was to find the
nests made of bits of cloth, newspaper and fur pulled from
the mothers' bodies. In her active imagination she was a
soldier who scooped up tiny, blind, hairless mice and
dropped them into a paper bag. They were ugly. Their
eyes had not opened, and their warm bodies were furless
with wrinkled pink skin. They pumped their little legs in
desperation when she plucked the helpless babies from
their smelly nests.

The soldier had no mercy. Her climb to the rafters of
the mill ended in exciting rides down the slides, sitting on

an empty burlap bag holding tight to the paper bag full of victims. She did not hesitate when she opened the bag and dropped the struggling little rodents into the canal located along the dike across the road from the mill. They were at war and it was her patriotic duty. The bag was folded and saved for the next expedition.

Levina recognized someone sitting in a car parked in front of the Chittenango Hotel on an autumn afternoon when they were walking home.

"Why, it's Grandma Hart," Levina said as she walked up to the car.

The old lady with curly gray hair rolled down the window.

"Look Phyllis, it's your Grandma Hart." Grandma Hart reached out to touch her granddaughter. Phyllis stepped back staring at the ground. She guessed she had met her grandma when she was little because she had seen a picture of them taken together, but she didn't remember her.

"Erwin is inside," Grandma Hart said raising her eye brows. Erwin had stopped for a quick beer and his mother did not approve. Grandma Hart had a lot to say, but the only thing Phyllis remembers was when she said, "I'm on your side, Levina."

"Daddy has a new farm," Levina said as they walked on down the sidewalk. "Grandma Hart lives with him."

"Why is she called Grandma Hart?"

"Because her second husband was Mr. Hart," Levina answered.

When the Christmas holiday was over, Phyllis went back to school and practiced writing 1944 on her assignment papers. That spring the allies invaded western Europe.

Aunt Marie stopped in often to talk about the war and their family members in Holland. The sisters put together boxes of food and soap and this and that for their Dutch relatives who were having a very rough time under Nazi occupation. One Sunday afternoon when Aunt Marie stopped in, Levina told Phyllis to run along. Phyllis assumed they were going to talk about stuff she wasn't supposed to hear. She hated secrets.

She went to Hazel's house, where they had chocolate milk and cookies. Phyllis said it would soon be her eighth birthday and proudly announced that England's Princess Elizabeth shared the same April 21 birthday.

"Hitler's birthday is the day before" she said, "I'm lucky that I don't have to share a birthday with him."

"Lucky," said Hazel.

"My friend, Nancy Lou's birthday is the same as Hitler's," Phyllis added.

"Poor Nancy," Hazel said.

"We always have birthday cake together. Our mothers, who used to be best friends, call us twins," Phyllis said. "It's just pretend," she added when Hazel looked confused. "Nancy lives in Oneida now, but her grandma lives across from the feed mill. Nancy and I play at her grandma's, but she won't let Nancy play with me in the mill. She says it's too dangerous."

Aunt Marie was waiting for her niece in front of the Baton house one late winter Friday afternoon when Phyllis arrived home from school. Levina had instructed her daughter to walk directly home that day

"Hurry," her aunt insisted, "your father is here."

Phyllis walked hesitantly into the kitchen where her mother and father sat talking. Aunt Marie did not follow her inside. Her parents smiled when she walked into the kitchen. She wondered what her father wanted. Maybe he told her mom about when she threw stones at the building.

"Hi, Babe." Her father smiled showing his pretty teeth.

"Hi," she said feeling shy.

"Do you want to go to Daddy's farm for the weekend?" Levina asked.

It was obvious to the seven-year-old that it was not really a question. They were going. Her suitcase was already packed.

Bowser and Phyllis were soon bundled into the back seat of her father's black Ford coupe for their first trip into the hills south of Chittenango to the little hamlet of Perryville. Levina was all giggly and giddy, and Phyllis felt left out. Bowser panted and his body trembled as Erwin drove down Falls Boulevard past the little building where he had seen Phyllis and Hazel throwing stones at the windows. Phyllis closed her eyes scooting down in the seat as far as she could, hugging Bowser and nuzzling his soft fur with her nose.

Six - 1944 - 1945

Phyllis, the Teamster

Standing behind her father on the empty manure sleigh Saturday morning, Phyllis tightened her arms around his slim waist as the team of dusty-chocolate colored work horses lurched forward. There was just enough snow on the ground for the wide wooden runners to glide smoothly over frozen field stubble. Bowser ran along the side of the sleigh, biting at snow as he tumbled along, seemingly happy to be back on a farm. Erwin used the sleigh every day during the winter to spread manure on his fields. He shoveled out the gutters after breakfast while the cows stood in the barn yard waiting to get back into the warm barn. Remnants of the early morning load were frozen to the sleigh so there was very little odor. There was no place to sit. Erwin pulled back on the reins to stay upright.

"Sleigh bells ring, are ya listening?" Singing was part of Erwin's normal conversation. He claimed that the only difference between him and the crooner Bing Crosby, was that Bing was famous. Erwin flicked the reins across the horses' backs, and the powerful muscles in their flanks rippled as they picked up the pace. Clouds of frozen breath from their huge nostrils curled around their heads like smoke.

Watching the horses, Phyllis let her mind wander. She had so many questions. First of all, she wondered what the heck was going on. She thought her parents were mad at each other, but last night they slept together. As usual, she was left to fill in the blanks of her own mystery story.

When they arrived at the farm house Friday afternoon, she had to pee really badly.

"Where's the bathroom?" she whispered to her mother who seemed flustered.

"There isn't one. You'll have to use a chamber pot or go to the outhouse," Levina whispered back.

"No bathroom? I want to go home." she whined. Levina shushed her daughter hoping her mother-in-law had not heard.

Standing at the kitchen coal range stirring home-made lemon pudding for her special pie, Erwin's mother, Grandma Hart, who kept house for her son, shook her curly gray head slowly back and forth, thinking that the child had a lot to learn about manners. She showed Phyllis to a small downstairs bedroom and pointed to a covered white porcelain pail. It was designed with a curved lip to make sitting more comfortable. A roll of toilet paper perched on the cover.

The only running water in the house came from an ugly black hand pump that stood over a dreadful black sink in the far corner of the dingy kitchen. Levina eyed it with disgust, wondering how Grandma Hart dealt with such primitive conditions. Most of the design was worn off ancient linoleum that would be impossible to keep clean. Levina shuddered. Grandma Hart had seen much worse conditions, and besides she didn't have uppity ideas like some of the younger generation.

A pot-bellied stove dominated the living room that was located just off the kitchen. Erwin opened the stove door and threw in a large chunk of wood. Sparks burst inside the stove like miniature fireworks. Puffs of smoke conjured up ghostly images as they escaped the stove and disappeared. Phyllis turned up her nose at the smell of smoke. She would come to appreciate the warmth of the big, old stove especially on cold winter mornings when she would stand close behind it to dress.

Soon after Phyllis's rude awakening about the primitive conditions of her father's house, Erwin escorted his wife and daughter to the barn to show off his herd of Holsteins. It had been almost two years since Phyllis had been inside a cow barn. She had forgotten about the smell.

"It stinks to high heaven in here."

"Shhhhh," her mother whispered.

A dozen and a half black and white dairy cows were stanchioned on either side of the barn floor with their rear ends hanging over manure-spattered gutters. One reddish-tan Jersey cow that was smaller than the others stood at the end of the row

"She's the one that gives us whipped cream," Erwin said. "Jersey cows' milk is richer in butter fat than Holsteins."

"She looks like Elsie, the Borden cow," Phyllis said. She wondered if her father was impressed that she knew about Elsie. He didn't act it.

"Watch out for Niagara Falls," Erwin yelled, laughing as his wife and daughter quickly side-stepped. Phyllis would learn not to depend on the accuracy of a cow's evacuation trajectory. When a cow, or several cows in unison, raised their tails that was the signal to move fast or be spattered with putrid cow urine.

"Hi," Phyllis said to the cows when she moved to the front of the stanchions. They stared at the girl with large, moist eyes and lashes to die for. Their muzzles were smeared with mash that they washed down with water from bowl-shaped fountains that were attached to water pipes between every other animal. Nose-activated levers released fresh water that they slurped into their mouths. They used their long tongues to clean out their noses.

The din of activity, the dairy barn cacophony, was a blend of radio music, the clatter of metal pails, cats mewing and hissing, cows rustling, munching, mooing, moving, eating, and slurping water, wood creaking, and straw rasping against concrete where the cows stood. It was a medley she would come to love.

Wooden stanchions swung open like very large safety pins when it was time for the cows to go outside. When they returned to the barn, each animal returned to its own place. They pushed their heads through the opening of the stanchion and Erwin closed the stanchion like a collar. Wood rubbed smooth by generations of bovine necks had a patina like fine furniture. At the end of the day, the cows lay in the straw, their heads still positioned in the stanchions contently chewing their cuds.

Erwin showed them the chicken house that was attached to the barn, asking Phyllis if she knew how to gather eggs. All she saw was the cantankerous big rooster who was eyeing her. Shaking her head in the negative, she hurried to the door. She couldn't get out of that place fast enough.

"Funny thing," Erwin said, poking his daughter to get her attention. "The former owners kept chickens in an upstairs bedroom in the house. That's what you call fresh eggs."

Erwin snapped the reins and clicked his tongue against the roof of his mouth in a clucking sound that startled his deliberative daughter. She opened her eyes and returned to the present. The horses pricked up their ears and strained harder in their harnesses, pulling the heavy sled to the top of the hill.

"Whoa," Erwin yelled, simultaneously pulling back on the reins. The horses' muscles rippled, rattling metal fasteners on their leather harnesses. They tossed their heads, snorting and straining to glance over their shoulders as if they wondered who the girl was. Most of Erwin's land was visible from the summit.

"That's it, Babe," he said with pride looking down on his farm, "my seventy acres. The land has a nice lie to it." Erwin felt satisfied that, at last, he was working his own land. Not that it was paid for, but it would be theirs someday if they worked hard. After Levina left, Erwin had taken the bull by the horns. Using his gumption as collateral, he convinced the right people that he was a

80

good investment. It wasn't the California chicken farm he had coveted; it was the best he could do. He was 44 years old. When his back hurt and exhaustion took over, he lamented that he was not getting any younger. He wouldn't live long enough to pay off the 20-year mortgage, but he gave it his best shot.

Grandma served Sunday dinner of roast ham, mashed potatoes, beets, cabbage salad, and lemon pie. Erwin fished into a quart jar of hot peppers with his fork and downed a slender red pepper as though his mouth was fire proof.

"Learned to love 'em in California," he said. "They cure what ails ya."

"We really need to be going," Levina said after she helped Grandma with the dishes. "I've got a lot to do at home."

Phyllis couldn't wait. She put on her coat and boots and hurried outside to find Bowser. He came running from behind the barn when she called, seeming just as anxious as she was to go home.

"The farm was awful," Phyllis told Hazel, holding her nose. "They don't even have a bathroom." Hazel could not imagine it. "The barn stinks. The gutters are full of cow poop and pee. When a cow raises her tail—look out. They spread their legs apart and it's like a stinky pee waterfall."

Her elation about being home was short-lived. Her father was gone when she got back to the house. Levina was smiling and happy, which was not her usual demeanor.

"Did you tell Hazel what a nice time you had?" Before Phyllis could answer, her mother said they were going back on Friday. From then on, visits to the farm were routine weekend events. Every Friday her father picked them up and every Sunday he brought them home. One Sunday Bowser was left at the farm. Neither Phyllis nor Bowser had been consulted. Her best buddy sat dejectedly beside the house watching the car head down the road without him. Phyllis and Bowser had never been separated before. Tears stung her eyes and she slid down in the seat so that no one could see her as Levina drove the car through Perryville and down the long hill to Chittenango.

When school ended in June, Phyllis and Levina moved to Perryville to live with Erwin. Phyllis missed Hazel and the mill where her mother still worked, but the good news was she enjoyed hanging around with her father who was good natured and fun. When farmer friends stopped in, Phyllis listened to the men swear and talk about cows and crops, equipment breaking down, and low milk prices. Erwin called her his "hired hand." She and her dad were buddies. She doesn't remember ever being spanked. Other kids said their parent's took switches to their breeches, but she guessed she was just lucky, because she wasn't always good. Sometimes her mother threatened corporal punishment, but Phyllis was faster on her feet, and had many secret hiding places in the barn.

Phyllis and her grandmother avoided each other. Grandma Hart didn't approve of her granddaughter thinking she was a spoiled little girl. Phyllis thought Grandma Hart had a mean expression on her wrinkled face. Phyllis hung out with her father and roamed the farm. Grandma sang hymns, and drank warm milk right from a cow that Erwin squirted into her cup. She drank it sitting on an old chair in the stinky cow barn.

"Yuck" Phyllis almost gagged. Once a week, Grandma fasted for a day, drinking only warm water with lemon juice. She sang hymns all the time and talked about heading up yonder. Her skin was funny like an old peach. Phyllis would have been surprised to hear that in time her skin would look exactly the same way.

Phyllis went happily about her chores feeding the cows and chickens, gathering eggs, and slopping the hogs.

"Don't get too attached to Ham and Bacon," Erwin said. Phyllis could not keep their names straight. They started out as cute little white pigs with curly tails and grew into big old hogs rutting around in the mud making weird snorting sounds. Phyllis didn't realize that first year what a terrible end was in store for the hogs.

At chore time just before evening milking, Phyllis gave each bossy cow a scoop of grist and a hand-full of salt on top of a portion of fermented corn silage that was warm from the silo. The chopped corn stalks cooked inside the silo, and smelled like sweet pickle relish.

"This is like dessert to the girls," Erwin said when he showed Phyllis how much grist to give each cow. He referred to the cows as "old bolognas" or "the girls." Sometimes he called them names that were not very nice. Then he would say, "Don't tell Ma." Phyllis loved the naughty way her father talked.

"Pretty soon you'll be climbing to the top of the silo, throwing down silage for poor old Pop," Erwin said. Watching him climb up metal rungs inside the wooden staved silo gave her a queasy feeling. "*Nope,*" she thought, "*not me.*"

"The silage is low this time of year," Erwin said. "Wait 'til you see how high it is after silo filling this fall."

The sound of horses' steel shoes echoed on the concrete barn floor as Erwin lead them, one at a time, out of their stalls when it was time for work. They lifted their tremendous hooves and plunked them down like they were too heavy.

Erwin picked up leather harnesses that hung on wall pegs in a precise way and placed them on each horse's broad back. Phyllis never tired of watching her father harness the horses, carefully arranging the leather straps, chains and clips. He hung heavy padded collars over their necks which allowed the animals to pull with their full weight and strength. Halters with eye-blinders were placed over their ears and secured around their necks. The semi-circle shaped blinders assured they could only look straight ahead and would not be distracted. He placed steel bits attached to the halters in their slimy hay-stained mouths and wiped his messy fingers afterwards on his overalls. The stuff from their mouths looked like hay vomit.

"Yuck." Phyllis liked the horses, but she could not imagine putting her hands in their huge, gooey mouths. The animals manipulated the bits with their teeth and large tongues, trying to find a comfortable position for the steel bit. Long reins used to steer the team were attached to each side of the bits.

Erwin flipped the reins and the horses that were harnessed together moved outside. He backed the team up to the hay wagon and attached the traces of the harnesses to a whiffletree, a pivoted horizontal crossbar that was attached to a long pole at the front of the wagon, one horse on each side.

"The old gray mare, she pooped on the whiffletree," Erwin said with a wink. The position of the horses' rear ends was just above the whiffletree. Phyllis got the joke and laughed. She didn't think her mom would approve of such talk.

Phyllis moved to the front of the team to pet their velvety soft muzzles. Flies buzzed around the horses' big, moist eyes and Phyllis shooed them away with her hands.

"You're my new teamster," Erwin told his confused daughter. She didn't know what a teamster was, but she soon found out. She got her first driving lesson standing next to her father.

"Say 'giddy-up' and thrust the reins along their backs and they move forward," Erwin said, showing her how to do it.

A tug on the left rein and the team turns left, right rein, right turn, pull straight back with a brisk "whoa" and they stop. Erwin handed his daughter the reins.

"Giddy-up," Phyllis said. Flicking the reins the team moved forward. Their flanks glistened with sweat as they pulled the wagon up the hill swishing their long tails from side to side like fly swatters.

"Damn things," Erwin said. "Makes you wonder why God created flies." The horses tried to reach the pests with their snouts, and twitched their hides from head to rump when the miserable things landed on their sweaty bodies. Phyllis figured the snorts and whinnies were horse language complaints to each other. They would get a good scoop of oats and grooming at the end of the day.

Phyllis enjoyed curry combing the horses with the metal gismo that did not look like any comb she had ever seen. She stood on an inverted wooden box, slipped her hand under the strap and slid the rippled groomer along the horses' backs like a sled. They snorted their appreciation.

Bob, Iva, and Eugene, their tall skinny teenage son, lived on the farm at the top of Hart's Hill that was named after them. Erwin's hilltop hay field was across from their house. Bob and Eugene wandered across the road for a neighborly visit the day of the embarrassing incident.

Erwin and Phyllis stood on the top of the load of loose hay. Phyllis held the reins, and Erwin said she could head to the barn. Bob unhooked the hay loader so Erwin wouldn't have to climb down off the load.

"Thanks," Erwin said, leaning on the hayfork that was stuck in the hay. "See ya later."

"Giddy yap," Phyllis said, pulling the reins to the left turning the team towards the barn. She felt very important driving the team all by herself. The proud little teamster was in the middle of the turn when she felt the hay rack tip, and she did as she had been told—she went with the load. Sliding off the topsy-turvy load as it hit the ground, she scrambled to her feet high tailing it down the hill with Bowser at her heels. Stopping just short of the barn, she looked back at the capsized load of hay and saw Eugene standing there with his arms in the air. She couldn't hear him but she could tell he was laughing. She had tipped over a load of hay and Eugene never let her forget it. In fact, he was still recounting the story 70 years later.

Phyllis got up off the lawn blanket where she was making up stories with her dolls when her mother drove into the yard. Something was wrong. She was crying.

"Where's Daddy?" she asked.

Phyllis ran to the barn to find Erwin followed by a disheveled sobbing Levina.

"The mill burned down," she sobbed. "Everything is gone. The fire was terrible with flames leaping toward the sky. The smell made me ill. Poor Ezra."

"What happened to the cats?" Phyllis asked, but she didn't get an answer. Levina was too upset to talk even if she had an answer.

"You should lie down, Ma," Erwin said, walking to the house with his arms around his wife's sagging shoulders.

"Finish the sweeping Babe," he said to Phyllis who went to the barn to finish sweeping the floors.

Life at the farm changed radically after the fire. Levina no longer had a job, and Grandma Hart got on her nerves. There was only room for one woman in Levina's kitchen, and that woman was Levina.

Phyllis peeked at Grandma Hart from behind a tree the day she left, not knowing what to say. Grandma sat in a straight chair on the lawn singing a sad song, "Always in the way, that is what they say," while she waited for her daughter, Gladys who lived a couple of hours away in Watertown to pick her up.

Grandma Hart moved to Florida, and eventually California. She made the rounds of her children's homes every year or so until she got too frail to travel. She went to be with the Lord in 1954.

Phyllis was curious about a bungalow nestled on the other side of the road just before Jay's house. She biked past it on the way to Perryville making up stories about who might live there. Perhaps it was a fairy godmother, a wicked witch, or a ghoul. The only way to find out was to ask.

"Who lives in the little house?" Phyllis asked one summer day after lunch.

"Rosie," Erwin said, and went back to reading his newspaper.

Sitting under the maple tree gazing down the road at Rosie's cottage with nothing to do, Phyllis and Bowser got curiouser and curiouser, just like Alice. Before long they meandered down the road and slithered through tall weeds to the back of the little house. Phyllis couldn't see anything over the weeds, but she could hear someone talking. She and Bowser moved slowly through waist-high tangled grass to the edge of an overgrown flower garden. A very small lady wearing a large straw hat over stringy gray hair was picking a bouquet.

"Hello?" Rosie looked toward Phyllis.

"Hi." Phyllis walked into view with Bowser at her heels.

"What's your name?" Rosie asked.

"Phyllis. This is Bowser."

Rosie reached down to pet Bowser who loved having his ears rubbed.

"You're a nice boy," Rosie said, "but my cat might not agree." Rosie lived alone with her cat Butch.

"Who were you talking to?" Phyllis asked.

"I was talking to the flowers. Don't you agree that one should ask a flower's permission before picking it?"

"I guess so," Phyllis said. It did seem like the polite thing to do.

Rosie showed Phyllis around her garden and soon they were chatting like old friends. Rosie snipped off a buttercup and held the flower under Phyllis's chin. A yellow reflection glowed on her skin.

"See that," Rosie said. "You like butter. Do you like to fish?" Phyllis hunched her shoulders.

"Don't know. Never tried it."

The next day Rosie introduced herself to Levina, saying she'd like to take Phyllis fishing. They were soon chugging down the road in Rosie's old car toward the Erie Canal in Canastota where they fished off a bridge.

"This canal has been here for more than 100 years," Rosie said. "It goes clear across the state from Albany to Buffalo, and years ago, it was filled with barges carrying all kinds of things. Some people even lived on their boats." Phyllis said she knew the song about "low bridge, everybody down." Having the history lesson behind them, Rosie introduced her to bullhead fishing.

"Bull heads are good eating," Rosie said as they stood by the canal with their fishing poles.

"My mother says they taste like mud," Phyllis said while she watched Rosie impale a wiggling worm's slimy body clear through twice on an ugly looking hook. She felt sorry for the worm. She held the fish pole patiently, tugging when she felt a bite the way Rosie showed her. After what seemed like forever, she caught a small wriggling bullhead. Rosie took it off the hook and Phyllis quickly threw the poor fish back into the muddy canal. Rosie laughed saying she was keeping hers.

On the way home in the car, Rosie talked about growing herbs and making a special tonic during lilac season.   Rosie's tall, old lilac bush occupied a large portion of her back yard.

"Lilacs have special curative powers. I make a mother essence by soaking lilac blossoms in pure spring water," she explained using her hands to accentuate the words. "To prepare the remedy for medicinal purposes, you combine three parts brandy, and one part essence in a medicine bottle."

When they got back to Rosie's house she showed Phyllis where she stored her remedy. A small brown glass bottle was kept inside the kitchen cupboard next to the salt and pepper.

"To settle the stomach and the spirit, you place a few drops under the tongue." Rosie demonstrated. "Works wonders."

Walking around the yard, she introduced Phyllis to her ancient lilac bush using formal introductions. Phyllis curtsied.

"Lilacs remind me of happy times," Rosie said. "They bloom in the spring—my favorite season." She rubbed her hand along one of the old branches. "In my opinion, no aroma in the world is more delightful than the fragrance of lilacs."

Phyllis and Bowser saw the farm pond for the first time on a hot July afternoon when Erwin asked them to perambulate up the hill to drive the cows down for milking.

"Head up the cow path to the woods near the pond," he said. "They'll be waiting for you."

Phyllis was anxious to find the pond and her imagination whirled excitedly as she and Bowser trudged up the pasture hill. Childhood was a time wreathed in sunshine. Nothing was impossible.

The herd rested under the shade of a small grove of large sugar maples on the hill above the pond that her dad said was God's fingerprint. They twitched their ears and tails at flies chewing their cuds in unison.

On hot summer days the cows spent the time between morning and afternoon milking's grazing and lazing in the woods. They kept track of the time with their udders. According to Erwin, a bulging bag of milk hurt like the devil. Usually, the herd loped along the path to the barn at milking time, but sometimes when the weather was hot and "the girls" were enjoying the shade, they ignored their discomfort and stayed in the woods.

When she got to the grove she could see water down below sparkling in the sunshine. She and Bowser dashed down the hill and walked across the cement dam that was located at the head of the reservoir. The pond had been used for harvesting ice before electricity.

Frogs croaked as she studied her blurred reflection in the water. Taking a cap pistol out of her pocket loaded with a brand new roll of caps, she shot a frog in play as a cap exploded. In reality she would never do such a mean thing. Some of the boys said they cut off frog's legs and threw the frogs back into the water. She felt sick just thinking about it. She had decided some time ago that most boys were mean.

Climbing back up the hill, Phyllis prodded the cows with a long stick, yelling: "Go on old bolognas." Bowser barked at their heels. The cows were in no hurry as they moseyed down the tree-lined lane to the barn. Their udders were swollen and milk leaked out of stiff teats on some of the larger bags that swung from side to side as they walked. Watching Phyllis stare at the cows' ample udders when they got to the barn, Erwin asked with a twinkle in his eyes if she thought they needed brassieres.

"The girls like it when I play with them," Erwin said as he wiped off the cow's udders with a clean rag before milking. Levina didn't like it when he talked like that, but Phyllis thought it was funny. He rubbed their bulging bags, talking to them in a calming way so they would let their milk down easily. He moved his three-legged stool from cow to cow, milking each one by hand. Resting his forehead on each cow's ample flank, he methodically pulled their teats two at a time, switching until all four were finally stripped of milk. Streams of warm creamy liquid hit the empty metal pail making a pinging sound that changed to a softer plop, plop, as the pail filled.

When the last cow was milked, Erwin poured milk into the cat dish while felines of various colors and sizes, clamored for a spot around the battered metal pan. Farm cats looked the same as mill cats, Phyllis observed, although they had a different smell. Mill cats had a musty, dusty smell, but barn cats smelled like manure. They washed themselves and groomed all the time, but they still smelled like the barn.

Phyllis went to sleep that night on the studio couch in the living room. The upstairs bedrooms were being painted. She woke up suddenly to whispering and a strange smell in the room. Sitting up, she peered through the archway into the next room where a light was on. Her mother was sitting on a pail and bloody rags were lying on the linoleum.

"Oh dear Lord," Levina sobbed. Erwin knelt next to his wife talking softly.

Phyllis retreated under her blankets. She guessed her mother had "come sick," with her monthly period. Levina had told her daughter that it happens to all women and not to be afraid. That night she was afraid for her mother who didn't usually cry when she "came sick."

Levina was crying the next morning when Phyllis peeked into her bedroom. She wondered why her mother wasn't getting up.

"We lost a baby. Please get breakfast for your Daddy. I need to rest before the doctor arrives."

So that was the problem, Phyllis thought, all of a sudden realizing that losing a baby caused bleeding. She thought about the bloody stuff that came out of a cow's behind after birthing a calf. She felt sad about the baby because she really wanted a sister.

After breakfast, Phyllis walked slowly toward the privy that was nestled under an over-hanging lilac bush carrying the covered slop pail they used during the night. Her mother usually took care of it, but that morning she was recovering from losing the baby. There was no sign of a baby. Phyllis wondered where it was.

Hinges creaked as she opened the door and stepped inside. Flies buzzed in the pit as Phyllis dumped the smelly contents of the pail through one of the round holes in the wooden seat. She filled a scoop with lime out of the open bag that was leaning against the wall and threw the white powder down the hole too. Lime kept down the smell. The farm privy didn't stink to high heaven like the mill outhouse.

In the mill privy, magazines and catalogs were used as toilet paper. The farm privy had toilet paper but catalogs were also piled in a corner. Phyllis borrowed the catalogs to cut out pictures of models and brought whole families of paper dolls together. Some of her catalog people had missing limbs because of the way they posed in their pretty clothes, but they were good company for the little girl. She named each doll and made up stories about their make-believe lives.

Hollyhock plants grew outside the privy like a miniature forest. Phyllis picked pink, white, and lavender blossoms to make hollyhock dolls. A large inverted blossom resembling a bouffant ball gown was the base. To that she attached a smaller blossom with a wooden toothpick to make the bodice. Buds comprised the head and arms. She spent hours playing with her flower ladies who attended fancy balls and had endless romances. The dolls only lasted one day, and they had to make time count.

Aunt Marie and Jerry (his mother called him Gerald) came to the farm on a Saturday morning to pack a box for Holland. Their Dutch relatives whose country was occupied by the Germans, needed just about everything.

Phyllis and Jerry roamed upstairs, and she showed her cousin the spooky little attic where the man with the yellow teeth lived. Only Phyllis could see him. The small garret was off the hallway at the top of the stairs, and you had to duck to get through the low door. Phyllis pulled the string to the bare light bulb that hung from the center beam. There were old things piled under the eaves: a pretty china pitcher and basin decorated with pink roses, suitcases, books, dusty boxes, and a photo album with funny looking people in old fashioned clothes.

They moved to the big attic at the end of the hall that had a window and was like a regular room except for bare beams and an unfinished, slanted roof. Phyllis wound up the Victrola and played her favorite old vinyl record, "Cannibal King," for Jerry. He thought it was silly. She told him golden deposits stuck on the beams was treasure. He said it was only sap. Jerry didn't have much of an imagination. When they got tired of attic games, they slid down the cherry wood banister really fast hitting the floor

93

a little too hard. Jerry skinned his elbow but refused to cry even though it hurt a lot. They weren't supposed to slide down the banister, so nothing was said.

"Who wants to color the oleomargarine?" Levina asked when Phyllis and Jerry walked into the kitchen.

"Me, me," they begged simultaneously. They both lunged for a thick plastic bag lying on the table that was stuffed with snow white oleomargarine. Phyllis grabbed it first. A tiny plastic capsule of oil-soluble food coloring was attached to a corner inside the bag. Phyllis pushed the red button, popping the capsule, and yellow coloring oozed into the white grease.

"Let me," Jerry insisted, grabbing the bag of margarine. Phyllis noticed, with a grimace, that Jerry had sores and blisters on most of his knuckles, and had lost his fingernails. She felt sorry for her cousin, but she was glad she didn't have the "condition," as bad as he and his brother, Kenny, did. They took turns kneading the oleomargarine inside the bag until it was a consistent yellow color. Levina said it was against the law to sell it colored because it looked too much like real butter and people might get cheated.

Phyllis watched reluctantly as the days of summer wound down. She would have to attend third grade in Perryville School. The two-story building that was built in 1897 as an Episcopal church, had a large open porch, an entry way with a Girls' toilet and a Boys' toilet and two class rooms downstairs. Daily classes were taught in one of the rooms. A fellowship hall and a kitchen were located upstairs. The church congregation used the upstairs room for Community Suppers and movies shown by the minister.

"I don't want to go," she pouted on the first day of school, "everybody will stare."

"You will be fine," Levina said as she drove to school and parked in the back of the building next to the swing set. They got out of the car and Levina noticed jam on Phyllis's face leftover from breakfast.

"Wait a minute," she said, spitting on her cloth hanky to wipe Phyllis's face clean. She escorted her worried daughter into the class room, spoke to the teacher, Miss Berman, patted her daughter's shoulder and left. Levina was in a hurry to get to her new teaching position at the one-room Bolivar School located just north of Chittenango. It was the answer to prayer; God's will. Levina had plans to modernize the farm kitchen with a new white sink and cupboard combination she had seen in the Sears catalog. It all took time—and money.

Kids were talking, whispering, laughing, sharing secrets, and ignoring the new girl. Standing where Levina had left her, Phyllis saw Mary, a girl she had known in first grade in Chittenango. She moved to Perryville to live with her grandparents.

"Hi," Phyllis said, feeling excited about seeing a familiar face, but Mary stuck out her tongue. Mary and Wilhelmina were sharing a banana, opening their mouths wide sloshing the mush around in their mouths, as if to say, ha, ha, we've got a banana and you haven't. Phyllis had a weak stomach, and almost gagged.

Miss Berman showed her to her desk. The class room included grades one through four; four rows of desks, one row for each grade with four or five students in each row. When she eased into her chair, a cute boy smiled from the second grade row. Feeling happy for the first time that day, Phyllis returned a shy smile before looking at the books on her desk.

"Everyone please stand," Miss Berman said. Placing their right hands over their hearts they faced the American flag and recited "The Pledge of Allegiance," then sat down wiggling and giggling.

"Quiet please," Miss Berman said. She asked them to bow their heads while she offered prayer.

After the opening ceremonies, Miss Berman introduced Phyllis. She then moved from row to row working with students in each grade. Older kids helped younger ones with reading and arithmetic. Phyllis read a story in the new Reader waiting for the teacher to get to the third grade students.

"How was school?" Erwin asked at the supper table.

"The kids are mean," Phyllis answered with a frown.

"This too shall pass," Levina assured her worried daughter.

"A cute boy named David was nice," she added.

"Sounds like you've got a boyfriend," Erwin chuckled.

"No," Phyllis said with a blush, "but he is cute."

Levina was usually right, and sure enough, before long Phyllis was accepted into the churlish group of country kids as one of the gang. Third and fourth graders huddled along the stone foundation during recess on a crisp October day. They shooed younger students away saying they were too little for the club. Mike, who drooled, shared a version of the nursery rhyme Jack and Jill to hoots of laughter from the boys.

"Jack and Jill went up the hill. They each had a dollar and a quarter. Jill came back with two and a half, but they forgot the water." A couple of boys giggled about stealing girls' cherries, whatever that meant. They laughed about the "F" word, but none of the kids dared to say that word out loud. Two scruffy boys, wearing dirty clothes that were too big for them, tried to edge into the group. Dark yellow mucous bubbled in and out of their nostrils as they breathed. Looking at the boys made Phyllis feel sick. They were poor and lived in a rusty trailer because their father was only a hired man.

"Snot faces, snot faces, snot faces," some of the other kids chanted in unison.

When the warning bell rang, the kids jumped up running along the gravel path encircling the school house, picking up speed with each revolution. Levina's admonition to be careful did occur to Phyllis, but she ran anyway, trying to keep up. She wanted to be like all the other kids, and she was until she stubbed her toe which sent her sprawling to the ground.

She hit hard and skidded along the gravel path. Feeling searing pain, she burst into tears. It wasn't as much about the pain as it was being embarrassed by ugly, raw sores. Her delicate skin peeled back on her wrists and knees, and bloody sores on her hands were embedded with dust, dirt, and gravel.

Mary helped her limp into the school house where Miss Berman administered first aid, washing and bandaging the wounds. Mary patted Phyllis's shoulder as tears stained her glasses.

"You'll live," Miss Berman said.

She couldn't wait to tell her mother about her injuries. She had another question too.

"What does 'knocked up' mean?" Phyllis asked her mother while she was peeling potatoes for supper. Levina hesitated and then said it had to do with a woman getting pregnant. So it's like the "F" word Phyllis thought, but she didn't ask for clarification.

Milkweed plants flourished along Erwin's hedgerows. The pretty pink and white flowers attracted Monarch butterflies who laid their eggs on the plants in the spring. Milkweed was the only food the caterpillars would eat. They were very clever eating bitter milkweed, because birds did not like the taste of bitter butterflies.

Levina showed Phyllis how to carefully pick a stem where a pretty pale green cocoon called a chrysalis with gold and black beaded stitching hung like a jewel almost out of sight. It was hard to understand how a caterpillar could create such a beautiful package just big enough to hold a folded up butterfly. They kept it in an old aquarium, and watched eagerly for the pretty butterfly to make its debut. The butterfly was yellow when it first hatched through metamorphosis (Phyllis called it magic) but as it dried it turned orange. Levina took it outside and it flew away. She had another one in her classroom.

The pretty star-shaped pink and white milk weed blossoms grew clustered together in bunches that looked like pompoms. The green seed pods that formed in the fall were shaped like tiny canoes. When they turned brown and dried, they split open, releasing thousands of brown seeds, each attached to its own beautiful silky soft white parachute.

Phyllis was on a mission on the autumn day when she headed up the farm hill, walking along the pasture fence with an empty burlap bag over her arm. She collected ripe milk weed pods that had not yet popped open and even some that had and stuffed them into the bag. It was her personal war effort. The silky threads attached to the seeds were as soft as down. The natural material was lightweight, had exceptional buoyancy, and was used to stuff military life vests and flying suits. Kids were encouraged by Uncle Sam posters to collect the pods and bring them to a post office. Phyllis imagined her milk weed silk saving the life of a brave pilot who was forced to ditch his airplane over the Pacific Ocean.

Phyllis came home from school to an empty house on a fall afternoon, and, as her mother would say, "bit off more than she could chew." The white enamel kitchen range was the center of the kitchen. It heated the room, cooked the food, and warmed water. Levina had waxed her eyebrows the night before, and left the small pan of

Zip hair remover on the back of the stove. Phyllis had watched her mother apply warm wax, wait a few minutes and quickly pull it off. She knew how to do it. She used a large match stick dabbing a small amount under her eyebrows.

While she was waiting, she checked the fire by inserting a curved steel handle with an end shaped like a claw into one of the iron disks on the stove top. Slowly lifting the heavy lid, she balanced it on the side of the stove cook top. Colorful flames danced and curled, and the hot lid tumbled to the floor scorching the rag rug that was spread in front of the stove. Impulsively, she grabbed the hot metal with both hands, burning every single fingertip. Jumping back in pain, she grabbed the handle and lifted the lid back on the stove. There was an ugly black scorch mark on Levina's nice rug. *"Boy will mom be mad,"* she thought. Eyes brimming with tears, she filled a bowl with cold water and fled to her bedroom. She sat on her bed soaking both hands, calling herself names like "idiot" and "dumb fool" between tears. Cold water was the only thing that eased the pain. She forgot about the Zip wax that was smeared under her eyebrows.

"Phyllis, you must learn to be more careful," her mother warned when she arrived home. Her burned fingers were sore, and the wax had dried too long. Pulling it off made her cry even more.

"Why do you use that stuff?"

"To be more beautiful," Levina answered. Phyllis didn't get it.

"Bath time," Levina called. Saturday night was bath night—the one and only weekly bath. The small, white enamel tub perched on a narrow table in front of the kitchen stove where it was warm. Phyllis stood on a chair to get into the tub that was partially filled with warm water heated on the stove. She felt like a big frog in a very small pond.

"Don't forget to wash 'possible,'" Levina instructed after scrubbing Phyllis's skinny back. She didn't need a reminder to wash her private parts. Mothers were funny.

Levina handed her daughter the washcloth, and went about her business leaving Phyllis to finish her bath. Sitting in the small tub with barely enough water to cover "possible," she fantasized about having a bathroom with a big tub like the one they had in Chittenango. She had no idea where her parents bathed. Certainly they didn't sit in the small tub on top of the table—did they?

Seven - 1945

The New Year brought encouraging news as the Allies continued to gain ground against Nazi forces. The daily *Syracuse Post Standard* newspaper came by mail, and Erwin caught up with war news sitting in his kitchen rocking chair after lunch. GI's dubbed the last great German offensive, "The Battle of the Bulge." The Nazis underestimated the Allied forces, and although the battle was long and bloody, the Allies triumphed. Maps of battle campaigns were printed in the newspaper.

Victory in Europe was in sight when on April 12 the country was stunned to hear of the death of President Roosevelt in Warm Springs, Georgia. The president, who had polio, and could not walk without assistance, died of a massive cerebral hemorrhage. FDR, as he was affectionately called, served three terms beginning in 1933 and ending at the beginning of his fourth term in 1944, the only U.S. president to have served more than two terms. Vice President Harry S. Truman became president.

On May 7, Germany signed its Instrument of Surrender. Victory in Europe, known as VE Day, and the end of the war in Europe, was a time for celebration.

"Now all we've got to do is finish off the Japs," Erwin said with concern. "And that could be a real problem."

Ten days after the U.S. detonated the world's first atomic bomb in the New Mexico desert, the Allies issued the Potsdam Declaration, demanding the "unconditional surrender" of all the Japanese armed forces. Japanese Prime Minister, Kantaro Suzuki, ignored the request.

On August 6, by order of President Truman, the U.S. B-20 bomber Enola Gay dropped an atomic bomb on the Japanese city of Hiroshima. Even then, the Japanese resisted unconditional surrender. Therefore, a second atomic bomb was dropped on the city of Nagasaki.

On August 12, Emperor Hirohito announced the Japanese surrender on national radio. Japan formally surrendered to the Allies aboard the USS Missouri in Tokyo Bay on September 2, 1945 ending World War II.

Mary rode to Phyllis's house on her brother's old bike that spring, showing off and bragging.

"I know how to ride a bike, and you don't," Mary chided.

"I don't care," Phyllis said.

"Want to try?" Phyllis was afraid of falling, but she was asking for a bicycle for Christmas, and there was no time like the present, her mother often said.

Mary grasped the back of the seat, running along beside the old bike as Phyllis struggled to balance. The front wheel wiggled out of control, and Phyllis slid off the bike many times before it hit the ditch. She was always worried about skinning her tender skin.

"You're clumsy," Mary laughed.

"You are just lucky having a brother to teach you stuff."

Mary suggested coasting downhill because then it was easier to balance. Phyllis practiced over and over, trying to coast from their house to Rosie's house. Then one miraculous day, it happened just like magic. All of a sudden she knew how to ride a two-wheeler!

"Success!" she yelled. Soon she was doing figure eights like a pro.

Levina's father, Grandpa VanDyke, came to live with them that summer while recuperating from stomach cancer surgery. He stayed with Aunt Marie for a while before moving to Perryville. Levina was worried about cancer germs. She scalded his dishes twice with boiling water and stored them separate from the other dishes.

Phyllis thought he had strange habits. It was amazing to a little girl the way he ate with his knife balancing vegetables on the blade. Phyllis looked away when he chewed gristle and sucked white marrow out of bones at the supper table, because it turned her stomach. He was strict about rules, but he was fun too. He told her on Christmas morning that he had heard noises on the roof during the night.

"Something up there scraped shingles," he said. Phyllis knew who it was.

Industrious to the end, Grandpa installed wood clapboards on the house, replacing ugly, gray asbestos siding. "See this," he said proudly in broken English, holding up a small piece of wood siding. "Only this much

103

left over. I figure good." Erwin said Grandpa was a good old guy.

Grandpa stayed in Perryville for the next few months and Phyllis had to adjust to his ways. One Saturday morning she was absorbed in "Let's Pretend," a children's radio drama, when her father came into the room asking for help in the barn.

"I'll do it after the story is done," Phyllis said. Erwin did not seem to mind.

"You go now," her grandfather chided. "Your father ask you do something—you do," he ordered. Phyllis was not happy, but she did it.

Aunt Marie, the best aunt in the whole world, had a special day planned that July. Ringling Bros. and Barnum & Bailey Circus was coming to Syracuse, and they were going. When Phyllis told her father they were going to the circus, he began to sing. Erwin had a song for every occasion. *He'd fly through the air with the greatest of ease, that daring young man on the flying trapeze. His movements were graceful, all girls he could please; and my love he purloined away.*

It was a cloudy day when Aunt Marie bundled Kenny and Jerry into the car. The boys, who were only 15 months apart in age, cuffed at each other just for the fun of it. Wesley and Bernice, Uncle Marinus's kids, sat quietly in the back seat.

"Why can't you two be well-behaved like your cousins?" Aunt Marie asked.

Phyllis sat on the rubber tire swing that hung from the largest branch of the old maple tree imagining elephants and tigers up close when Aunt Marie pulled in the driveway. Jerry had to go to the toilet and then they were off. Levina was worried about the storm clouds.

In Syracuse, Aunt Marie parked in a big field near the railroad tracks and urged the children along walking against the wind that turned her umbrella inside out.

Inside the big top silly clowns ran around all in a dither and acrobats did cartwheels in a parade with pretty girls riding elephants. Prancing horses pulled fancy wagons with bars that held tigers and the strong man lifted weights like it was nothing. At last Phyllis understood why it was called a "three-ring-circus." There was so much going on all at once she didn't know where to look. Trapeze artists dazzled the crowd jumping from swing to swing terrifying the audience with their daring performance. Phyllis couldn't wait to tell her father she had seen "the daring young man on the flying trapeze."

The Greatest Show on Earth was all glitz, glitter and cotton candy fun until an uninvited guest became the most prominent participant. Canvas flapped and sagged as wind whipped through the big top, and noisy, pelting rain nearly drowned out the band. The great tent heaved and shuddered.

"Everybody out," the ring master yelled in a booming voice through a megaphone. "Please proceed slowly toward the nearest exit." Aunt Marie said they had to go and they stepped carefully down wooden bleachers until they were on the ground. Looking over their shoulders they saw circus performers heading out of the tent in the opposite direction. They dashed toward the parking lot past concessions, food tents and games leaving the circus behind.

"I tried," Aunt Marie said, "I really tried; but don't worry, someday we'll come to the circus again."

Phyllis took her own children to Cole Brothers Circus, but it was 2010 before she treated two of her grandchildren to the Ringling Bros. Barnum and Bailey Circus. By then the circus had moved inside. The big top was gone, and so was some of the magic.

105

Levina said that Stella was a "big frog in a small pond." Phyllis had no idea what that meant, nor did she realize the statement was a clue to her mother's true personality. Levina saw herself as a leader, and Stella was competition. One of Stella's accomplishments was organizing "The "Builder's Club," a youth group that met one Saturday a month at Stella's little house at the top of the hill on the way to Chittenango. Stella was active in the community and walked with a self-confident swagger. Her husband, Harley, reminded Phyllis of Uncle Remus in one of her books. Harley was white and Uncle Remus was black, but to her they looked alike.

It was a brisk fall day when Phyllis and Alan met by chance at the school house corner on the way to a Builder's Club meeting.

Heading west, they strolled past the Red and White Grocery store where kids bought ice cream and hung out on the wide, pockmarked concrete platform along the front of the building. The store was open Monday through Saturday, and closed on the Lord's Day.

They stopped for a minute on the cement bridge over the road to throw stones in the creek that rushed on towards Perryville Falls.

"Let's look at the mill pond," Alan said turning left and walking up the short dirt road that dead-ended at the pond. Water run-off from Fenner hills formed a small creek that trickled into the pond. A waterfall at the edge of the pond had in years past powered a water wheel for the grist mill that ground grain for local farmers. Standing by the old stone foundation, Phyllis imagined the creaky old moss-covered wheel revolving in a steady rhythm.

"Hear that?" she asked.

"Hear what?" Alan asked.

"The creaking of the old mill wheel."

"You're nuts," he said.

Walking back along the road toward Stella's, they stopped at the small white church for a few minutes to sit on the front steps.

"Are you saved?" Phyllis asked.

"Saved? Saved from what?"

"Your sins."

"I don't know. I guess so."

"I haven't seen you in Sunday School lately," Phyllis said, feeling a little worried about Alan's soul.

"Are you?" Alan asked.

"I must be. My mother is."

Levina had been designated as a born leader in her high school year book, and she took that charge very seriously. Church leadership took priority. Every single Sunday she laid out her husband's under wear, socks, dress shirt and neck tie on the bed, and hung his only suit over the door. The only valid reason to miss church service was illness.

The church bell echoed from the village all the way to the farm as they got in the car.

"Come, come, come, come, come to the church in the wildwood, " Erwin serenaded his family as they drove to the small village church.

Sunday church service was a social gathering as well as a time for worship. Everyone knew everyone. Levina made the rounds before the service, walking to where people sat in their pews waiting for the service to begin, with bits of important information; or so it seemed. Levina taught Sunday School, and later served as superintendent. She was an outspoken member of the Women's Society for Christian Service (WSCS), and attended   weekly bible study. She chaired many committees, served on the administrative board, and was unofficial liaison between the pastor and the membership. Erwin was active in the Men's Brotherhood.

Levina enjoyed entertaining the pastor for Sunday dinner; keeping him up to date on community happenings. Pastors in the Methodist Church changed quite often, and Levina was always the first lay person to introduce herself.

Phyllis went to Church and Sunday School where she pestered teachers with questions they couldn't answer. If Adam and Eve and their sons Cain and Abel, were the only people in the world, where did Cain's wife come from? She never got an answer.

"Let's go," Alan said, not wanting to pursue the saved question.

"Did you know church walls can talk?" Phyllis asked as they got up and continued their walk to Stella's.

"That's silly," he said.

"No it isn't. They really do."

Since 1839 the white clapboarded Methodist Church had stood along the main drag in the center of the village. A belfry housing a bell squatted on the roof. Old folks remembered the wind storm that took down the steeple. White haired old ladies in missionary circles said the church could tell a heap of stories if only the walls could talk. Sitting in church every single Sunday, Phyllis visualized the walls with wide, grinning mouths spewing all kinds of gossip. She was pretty sure she was the only one who heard the whispering walls.

No one else showed up for the Builders Club meeting that day. Stella gave them each a small paper bag of cookies and sent them on their way.

"My dad calls Perryville a one-horse town," Phyllis said, as they headed back down the hill into the village.

"What does that mean?"

"I don't know, but my dad is never wrong." Phyllis answered. "He lived in California."

"Wow!"

"Look. There's the old fortress," Phyllis said pointing north across the fields at the Worlock Stone Quarry complex.

"What do you mean, a fortress? That's the quarry," Alan countered.

"You don't have any imagination." Phyllis scowled.

The "main drag" as Erwin called the paved road, ran west to east or vice versa, through the village with eight additional roads angling off in every direction; two were paved, six were dirt. Three of the dirt roads had no outlet. Forty or so houses of various sizes and a trailer or two, lined the main drag; large homes with spacious porches, medium sized homes, and bungalows in various stages of disrepair, two general stores, a church, and the unpainted IOOF Hall. The school house was perched on a rise where the road split in three directions. A few people kept up their houses but the majority of homes were in need of paint. Century old maple trees lined the road; sidewalks heaved and buckled from encroaching roots.

The village was oddly located in three separate townships, Sullivan, Fenner and Lincoln. The Lambert's farm was located in the township of Lincoln, and for that reason, Erwin and Levina voted in Clockville. Dairy farms dotted scenic, rolling hills in every direction surrounding Perryville.

Hill's General Store and Post Office, the size of a small barn, was the largest building in town. Just past Hill's store Coon Road wound its dusty way north past a house or two and crumbling foundations that stood near the Lehigh Valley Railroad tracks. The train still passed through the valley twice a day, but it no longer had any reason to stop. Decades earlier, Perryville had been a bustling shopping hub for surrounding farms. The Lambert's unkempt neighbor Jay, had informed Phyllis about drunkards buying pails full of beer at the saloon that sloshed over the top as they walked. He fancied himself somewhat of a local historian, but Levina said that was debatable.

"Let's go to the falls," Phyllis suggested, picking up the pace along Coon Road. "Maybe we'll see the train."

Canaseraga Creek was fed by tributaries of numerous springs from the northern slope of the Fenner watershed that supplied the mill pond and the creek. The creek plunged 150 feet into the spectacular steep rock basin of Perryville Falls, and that's where Alan and Phyllis headed.

The two adventurers skidded down a steep dirt trail to the bottom of the soaring waterfall, grabbing bushes for support, and muddying their shoes and the seats of their pants. Rushing water roared and plunged over the falls onto the rocks below. Struggling back up the trail was more challenging than sliding down. Back at the top they followed the railroad tracks that headed straight to Canastota passing along the edge of old Jay's cow pasture.

"Let's go to our pond," Phyllis said with a spurt of excitement. Alan said okay and took another bite of one of Stella's good sugar cookies.

They plodded through Jay's pasture, and crossed the road at the top of the hill walking along a stone wall to the Lambert pond. They had no idea how long they had been wandering, and being kids, they didn't realize their parents were worried. Alan ate his last cookie and blew up the bag making a loud pop. Phyllis still had cookies in her bag.

Back in civilization, Levina telephoned Stella when Phyllis didn't arrive home at the usual time. Stella said they left her house around two o'clock. Levina panicked. She telephoned the state police and the Perryville boy scouts were mobilized for the search. Resident phoned resident all over town. Had anyone seen them? Finally, someone remembered seeing two people, cross the road at Jay's hill. One of them was wearing a red coat.

"My word," said Levina, "Phyllis is wearing a red coat. "

When Erwin heard they were seen crossing the road on Jay's Hill, he was pretty sure he knew where they were.

"Damn. Why didn't I think about the pond before," he said, hurrying up the hill through the cow pasture.

The sun hung low in the western sky, and the explorers were standing on the dam when Alan saw Phyllis's father walking fast heading their way. Alan did an about face heading cross lots in the opposite direction.

"Not so fast young man!" Erwin marched the errant children down the hill to the house. Alan's mother, Alberta, was at the Lambert's waiting for some word of her missing son. Levina was so happy to see them that all she could do was cry and hug her daughter. Her mother was not much of a hugger, and Phyllis knew this time she had gone too far. Grandpa VanDyke was hopping mad.

"Whip her, Levina. She needs a whipping."

"I can't. I'm just so glad to see her," Levina answered. "So glad."

For years, Perryville people told the story about the day when Phyllis and Alan ran away together. It was, of course, an exaggeration. All they had intended to do was take a walk.

The next morning in the barn Phyllis's father was still teasing her about having a boyfriend. She said Alan was definitely not her boyfriend. Phyllis held open a burlap bag as her father stuffed kittens in the bag. The kittens were squealing and scratching, and Erwin, who wore thick gloves as protection against razor-sharp claws, was cussing.

Every now and then he took male kittens to his friend Asa's farm just down the road toward the quarry, to be neutered. Cats in the barn kept down the mouse population, but there were just too many of them. In Asa's barn, the old man unceremoniously stuffed their heads in a section of stove pipe and quickly snipped off the family jewels. Asa said it only hurt for a minute, but by the sound of the squealing tom cats, it was a very painful minute. Erwin made Phyllis wait in the car.

Phyllis woke up one cold November Saturday dreading the day. Erwin's friend, Jim, from Chittenango was coming up to stick the hog. One hog would be butchered and one sold. Jim arrived in good spirits. He had a booming voice and a friendly, handsome face. Phyllis could not understand why such a happy man wanted to kill hogs. She stayed inside but she could still hear the animal's frantic squeals. She clasped her hands over her ears as tight as she could hoping to shut out the death screams of the animal she had fed and watered since spring. She thought about how happy the hogs were to see her every day with the pail full of food. They crowded the fence in anticipation, stepping in the trough and staring at Phyllis with beady little eyes. And now they were going to eat one of them.

She pressed her hands tighter against her ears, and then everything was quiet. Soon the decapitated, disemboweled carcass was hanging upside down on a sturdy limb of the old maple tree in the back yard. Erwin and Jim stood next to the carcass, smiling as though they had managed some special feat, while Levina took a picture.

Phyllis stared at the macabre head with cloudy eyes, floppy ears and bristles on the snout cooking in a big pot on the kitchen stove. Levina sliced cooked meat off the head, mixing it with spices and packing it into a crock sealed with lard that would be stored in the cool cellar until her parents sliced it for sandwiches. Levina's canned pork was the tastiest meat in the world, but Phyllis would not touch head cheese.

Eight - 1946 Part One

Best Friends
Phyllis and Betty

Phyllis woke up every morning that spring to the disgusting sound of her mother gagging and retching. Feeling her own stomach turn, she clasped a pillow over her ears to muffle the sound. Had her mother caught cancer from her grandfather? Levina always scalded his dishes with boiling water, but Phyllis worried.

"Don't worry," Levina said, "I'm okay." Phyllis was confused. How could her mother be ok when she threw up every single disgusting morning?

"We're going to town," Erwin said after lunch on a warm July day, "so put on your traveling togs."

Bowser watched with his head tilted and one ear slightly up, listening as they got into the car. Phyllis knew he wanted to hear her call his name. He never wandered far. He would be waiting.

Phyllis paced the sidewalk outside the green and yellow John Deere tractor store next door to the State Bank of Chittenango where Erwin parked the car. She could see her father through the large plate glass window, talking and laughing with a man in the store. Levina was at Dr. Boyd's office further down on the other side of Genesee Street. Phyllis kept watch running to meet her mother as soon as she came out of the doctor's office that was in a wing of the house.   Phyllis remembered attending a birthday party for Dr. Boyd's daughter, Jill, at the house when she lived in Chittenango.

"Let's wait for daddy in the car," Levina said.

"Are you all right?" Phyllis asked once they were seated in the Ford.

Levina hesitated before she spoke looking directly at her daughter with one of her serious, worried expressions.

"Phyllis, I'm trying to have a baby." Levina had suffered two miscarriages and doubted that she would be able to carry this baby.

"We're going to have a baby?

"We're trying," Levina repeated. It was an answer to Phyllis's prayers. She had wanted a sister forever.

"It won't be until next winter," Levina said. "We need to be patient."

Phyllis was excited about the baby, but that day she wanted to get back home to ride her new bicycle. Some mornings when she woke up she ran to the tool shed to see if her beautiful bike was really there. It seemed too good to be true.

The summer before, Grandpa VanDyke had returned to Canastota Hospital because the cancer was back. Levina reminded Phyllis every night to remember Grandpa in her prayers. He was the only grandpa she ever knew. Erwin's father, Joe Lambert, died in the "poor house," Erwin said, just before Phyllis was born. Phyllis did pray, but she decided Grandpa's recovery was not God's will. He died on February 10, 1946 at age 66. Phyllis felt sad that she couldn't attend the funeral. She had never been to a funeral, or seen a dead person.

Iva came down from their hill to sit with Phyllis who was confined to her darkened bedroom with a bad case of German Measles. Dr. Cannon stopped in on his rounds, and reminded Iva to keep the blinds drawn. People could go blind from measles unless their room was kept dark. Phyllis was so sick all she wanted to do was sleep.

"Phyllis, I have something to tell you," Levina said after a visit to Stickles Law Office in Chittenango for the reading of Grandpa's will a few months later.

"Your grandfather was very generous. He left each of his grandchildren $50.00."

"Fifty Dollars!" Phyllis exclaimed. "What luck!" She had wanted a bicycle forever but they were expensive and, as her father often reminded her, they were poor. Erwin enjoyed exaggerating. They certainly weren't rich but they weren't poor either. They had their own farm. They were not white trash.

"Thank you Grandpa! Thank you!" Phyllis couldn't wait to buy a bike. Grandpa was. even better than Santa Claus.

Piles of dirty snow melted slowly and spring inched in. Tulips, daffodils, peonies and lilacs came and went. Trees sprang to life in delicate greens. Phyllis picked out a snazzy red and white bicycle in the Sears, Roebuck and Company Catalog. The bike had a battery-operated light, a real horn, and a basket. Then one wonderful day Erwin and Levina drove her to the Sears store in Syracuse to pick up her bike.

"I got it! I got it!" she told Betty over the phone. "Can you come down?" Betty's mother, Edna, drove her down the hill to Perryville. Phyllis could not stop smiling. Levina took a picture of the best friends with Phyllis's new bicycle.

School ended for the summer, the most special summer ever because of her new bicycle. Chores came first: helping her mom clean the house and working with her dad in the barn. She fed the cows, pigs, and chickens, gathered eggs, and shoveled gloppy manure out of calf pens. She played her imagining game the whole time, talking out loud inventing romantic adventures.

Speeding quarry trucks double clutched up Jay's hill as Phyllis pedaled hard past Rosie's house trying to make it to the top of the hill. After getting to the school house, she pushed her bike most of the way up hill to Betty's house. As it turned out, Betty wasn't home and Phyllis coasted all the way back feeling free as a gypsy.

Second choice to bike riding was her secret world of romantic fantasy. She gathered inspiration for characters in her stories from radio soap operas that Levina listened to on her kitchen radio while preparing supper. Fifteen-minute episodes of: *When a Girl Marries, Portia Faces Life, Just Plain Bill,* and *Old Ma Perkins*, transformed the Lambert's stark farmhouse kitchen into a theater. Phyllis listened closely, absorbing convoluted details about unrequited love and heartbreak while she reclined on the cot that was pushed against the outside wall of the large kitchen. Her dolls took on personalities of leading characters.

A Farnsworth floor model radio was their entertainment center bringing news, mysteries, romantic drama, variety shows and concerts into the living room. Levina, who firmly believed that idle hands were the devil's workshop, sat darning socks. She slipped a wooden darning egg inside Erwin's holey work socks to keep the material firm while she weaved smooth patches over worn spots.

The creaky door opening of the radio show *Inner Sanctum Mystery* gave Phyllis chills in a fun way. She rode across the western plains with the Lone Ranger and Tonto, and visited fairy tale locations with *Let's Pretend* every Saturday morning, retreating happily into her fantasy world. Playacting was entertainment. She had a romantic temperament and especially enjoyed making up love stories with herself as the heroine.

On pleasant summer days her playground was a shady place along the creek that rushed downhill from the pond and twisted through the cow pasture. Bowser followed his girl, chasing rabbits and sniffing out woodchucks.

Phyllis and Bowser explored the woods, a small grove of trees, not a proper forest, but it worked for all the imagining Phyllis conjured. Lying on her stomach on the warm cement dam, she studied water creatures: crabs, minnows, pollywogs in the spring and the frogs they became, slim snakes the size of horse hairs that wiggled and twisted like real sea serpents, and yucky black leeches that the kids called blood suckers.

The pond was the best imagining place on earth as far as Phyllis was concerned. She felt safe there. She could be herself and no one would make fun of her. Overgrown grape vines clung to trees south of the water like the vines Tarzan used swinging through the jungle in movies and comic books. She heard Tarzan's yodeling yell echoing through the woods.

Phyllis's upstairs room faced the back yard with a view of the barn. Her bedroom windows were open, and night breezes carried the sweet smell of drying hay and night noises into her room. July was nearly over, and she was thinking about school starting again when she heard a car pull into the driveway.

Levina, who always walked fast, dashed from the living room to the kitchen to switch on the outside light. Through the upstairs window, Phyllis watched a man with a suitcase get out of the car and walk across the back yard to the kitchen door.

Phyllis moved slowly down the tall stairway sliding her hand along the smooth, wide, cherry wood banister that curved into a rosette at the bottom of the stairs. She walked through the living room and dining room and waited at the kitchen doorway, watching a short, muscular man with curly gray hair give Levina a big squeeze. Phyllis's parents did not hug or kiss in front of her, and Phyllis was surprised to see her mother in the man's arms.

"It's your Uncle Harry from Florida," Levina said with a weak smile. Uncle Harry moved toward his niece with a look that made her feel uncomfortable.

"Who's this big girl? I haven't seen you since you were a little tyke." She stepped back. "What's this? Aren't you gonna give your old Uncle Harry a hug? I like little girls."

Phyllis was not the least bit interested in giving the man a hug. She didn't even hug her father. She glanced

119

at her mother who nodded "yes." Feeling embarrassed dressed only in a night gown and panties, she put her arms loosely around his neck when he picked her up. He squeezed her so tight it hurt and patted her bottom when he put her down.

"Back up the golden stairs," Levina said. "It's past your bedtime." The grown-ups laughed as she climbed the stairs, and, as usual, she wondered why they were laughing at her.

The next morning at breakfast, Erwin talked with Uncle Harry about the carpenter work he had been hired to complete in the church sanctuary. Erwin had recommended his older brother for the job of installing new wallboard. Harry would be staying with them for a few weeks until the job was done.

Summer moved languidly on. Phyllis did her chores, helped Erwin in the hay fields, went fishing with Rosie, and rode her bike to the store to meet friends, always hoping David would be there. He spent a lot of time out of town with his grandfather. When he was home, he drove to the farm to see her, and they sat together in Sunday School. She wrote stories about a different exciting life. She made big plans for herself, big plans that she didn't share with anyone. In her best day dreams, she was a newspaper reporter like her favorite comic strip character, beautiful Brenda Starr.

One morning Erwin came in for breakfast carrying a white puffball the size of a basketball that he found growing in the pasture. He set the edible fungus next to the kitchen sink, saying it would be good fried up for lunch. Phyllis was amazed how something as tasty as a puffball could grow so fast. They seemed to sprout up overnight. She believed puffballs were the manna the Jews found when they were wandering in the wilderness. She wondered if they, too, fried them in butter.

120

Uncle Harry fingered the puff ball flicking off dried cow manure then chuckled saying he didn't know as though he wanted to eat an overgrown mushroom that grew in the cow pasture.

"I did a damn good job at the church, even if I do say so myself," Uncle Harry bragged. "I should finish up today."

Phyllis was glad to hear it. She was anxious to have her family back to herself.

"Hey, Ma," Erwin said, "There's an old cluck strutting around the hen house. I'm kinda hungry for chicken dinner." Erwin left for the barn and Harry sidled up to Levina whispering in her ear as she worked at the kitchen sink. She moved away from him nervously wiping her brow with the hem of her apron.

"I need to see about that hen," she said.

"How's my girl?" He turned to Phyllis. She wanted to say that she was not his girl, but knew better than to sass back. Instead, she mumbled "good," then slid away from the table, saying she had to gather eggs. In truth it was too early in the day to gather eggs, but she would check the nests anyway.

"I'll go with you," Levina said. She needed to cull out the "old cluck" for dinner.

Broody hens had a different demeanor than laying hens and were easy to spot. They puffed their feathers and made low clucking sounds, "pluck, pluck, pluck," or sat with their feathers all puffed up in a nest as though they were protecting a family of chicks.

Levina found the broody hen in one of the nests and grabbed her quickly by her legs despite desperate squawks of disapproval from the hen. Broody hens stop laying eggs when they are intent on hatching chicks, and when a hen stops earning her keep, she is destined for the stew pot.

Reaching under a hen in a nest checking for eggs, Phyllis was startled to find an egg that was soft like an under inflated balloon. She handled it gently placing it carefully in the basket until she could show her mother. It was a mystery; some goofy hen playing a joke.

The chickens were allowed free range during the day, and lucky for Phyllis that day there was no sign of the mean rooster who her father said "keeps the hens happy." Phyllis didn't understand why he said that. She didn't often ask questions, but she didn't agree. She watched uneasily when the big bully chased hens around the barn yard raising all kinds of dust and commotion. The chosen hen ran and dodged until he cornered her and scrambled onto her back grasping her feathers with his claws and his beak. At that point the poor hen usually gave up, crouched and waited, but they did not look happy. When he jumped off and swaggered away, the hen made a production of shaking herself in what Phyllis thought was relief. Anyway, the rooster seemed to upset the hens and he scared Phyllis to death when he gave chase. If he came within a few feet of her, she threw cracked corn to distract him and then ran for her life.

Erwin and Harry stood by the tool shed talking when she left the barn with the basket of eggs. Erwin was leaning on his big scythe getting ready to wage his private war against weeds. He kept the 30-inch blade of his scythe very, very sharp with a grinding wheel that shot sparks as he honed the scythe. He carried a whetting stone to sharpen the scythe as he worked

"It has to be sharp enough to cut butter," Erwin said. Phyllis did not realize until years later that watching her father was like watching an artist at work. He made the scythe dance in a flawless motion of perfect symmetry. (*Erwin's scythe is one of Phyllis's treasures.*)

Phyllis went around the barn in another direction to avoid walking past the men. Just then they burst into rude

122

laughter. She caught up with her mother at the chopping block located under the tall, overhanging lilac bush. Levina placed the hen's head on the chopping stump, holding the docile bird by the feet with her left hand. Why the doomed chicken did not struggle at this point was a mystery to Phyllis. It was always the same; hens accepting their fate without a struggle. Holding the sharp axe with her right hand, Levina skillfully beheaded the hen with one swift chop.

A cat crept out of the weeds, grabbed the bloody head and skittered away with the prize. Levina released the decapitated bird on the ground. The headless body writhed and twisted in a death dance as blood spurted from its jagged neck. When the bird stopped flopping around, Levina tied twine around its legs and hung it upside down from a sturdy lilac branch. Blood dripping from the neck coated the grass making it dark and slick. Another barn cat licked the grass as blood dripped on its head.

The decapitation process was routine, merely a part of farm life. Phyllis didn't even wince, although she said a little prayer for the hen. When Levina was ready to pluck the chicken, she held the headless bird upside down by its legs and dipped the body in a pail of hot water. Phyllis helped pluck, but she hated the way wet feathers smelled and stuck to her fingers.

In the kitchen Levina dressed the hen on the table that was covered with layers of newspaper, skillfully cutting the carcass open with a sharp butcher knife, and removing the viscera. She was very careful not to puncture the bile sack which could ruin the meat. Her hands were covered with blood and flesh, and a strong slaughter house odor permeated the kitchen. She scooped out under-developed yolks of various sizes that were clustered together and saved them for baking. She deftly cut the hen in neat pieces: drumsticks, thighs, wings, and breast and cooked

them in a pot with vegetables. The gizzard, the hen's
stomach, was turned inside out, and partially digested
grain and grit rinsed away.   Since chickens do not have
teeth, they swallow gravel to pulverize the grain they eat.
During the winter, when they were confined inside, the
chickens ate crushed oyster shells for the same purpose.
The back, neck, gizzard, heart, and liver were boiled to
make broth.

Phyllis's special imagining place, a kingdom all her
own, was along the creek where huge elm trees grew,
their gnarled roots clutching the creek bank like long,
witches' fingers.   The woody appendages formed a
narrow shelf where Phyllis sat.   Her long, dark braids
tickled her cheeks as she leaned forward peering into the
water. Pushing up her glasses that slid down her moist,
freckled nose, she wanted to toss the annoying things into
the stream.   Silvery water swirled around smooth, mossy
rocks before plunging on toward the cool culvert under
the road where her cave people lived. Scooping up damp
clay that day on her way to the elms, she molded
primitive pottery now drying on a flat rock in the summer
sun.
Shifting her position, she sat with her back against a
tree with her long legs hanging over the creek.   She
didn't like being the tallest kid in fourth grade, but her
dad laughed when she pouted.
"You're like a spring foal," he told her. "That's why
we call you Philly. And if you don't stop pouting, your
face is liable to get stuck like that."
A shy, gawky girl, Phyllis was most comfortable by
herself. Her pet cemetery was located nearby on a high
spot where the creek split and formed a tiny island. Small
graves of countless barn kittens were marked with crude
crosses made from fallen branches tied together with
brown twine from bags of cow feed. The life of a barn cat

was tenuous at best. Many were strays who wandered into the warm barn and stayed. Tom cats moved from barn to barn and females gave birth every three or four months. Phyllis searched the hay mow for half-wild kittens that spat and clawed when she picked them up. She tried, not always successfully, to keep their needle-sharp claws away from her tender skin.

Kittens left the hay mow, searching for food when their mothers stopped nursing them, and often could not find their way back to the safety of their birthplace. The herd was oblivious to their existence. After a meal of warm milk, kittens often curled up in bedstraw under the cows when the animals were standing. Cows do not lie down gently and when they plopped heavily into the straw, the result was, as Erwin said, "flat cats." He callously picked up the little corpses with his pitchfork tossing them on the manure wagon. If Phyllis saw them first, they got a decent burial. Sometimes Phyllis found entire litters with their necks broken lying in the haymow, presumably killed by a jealous tom cat. Female cats had no interest in suitors when they had kittens, and the toms knew it. Winter kittens often caught distemper and Phyllis washed yellow mucous out of their tiny eyes using pieces of cotton flannel dipped in warm water with dissolved boric acid powder. In spite of her tender mercies, not all of them survived the disease.

Closing her eyes, Phyllis began another oral chapter of her cave people saga, weaving the details in her mind and speaking in individual voices of various characters. She was completely engrossed in her make-believe world and wasn't aware that Bowser had wandered off following a scent that only he could smell. Someone else had arrived.

"Who ya talking to?" She was startled, and then felt embarrassed when she saw Uncle Harry standing nearby.

"To my story people," she said wondering how he had found her special place.

"How about showing me that famous pond," he suggested, holding out his hand to help her up the creek bank. She glanced toward the house hoping to see her mother.

"Who ya lookin' for? Everybody's busy. Come on."

Reluctantly, she followed him, walking along the dusty cow path up the pasture hill. Erwin's young stock made munching sounds as they grazed, moving from spot to spot, avoiding dried cow manure. A young bull smelled around the tail of one of the females. Uncle Harry noticed and laughed.

"Do you know how babies are made?"

Of course she knew about cows and bulls mating, did he think she was stupid?

"Cow's babies are called calves," she said.

A small brown rabbit darted from under a thorn apple bush and scurried across the path, disappearing into the thicket along the barbed wire fence. She wished she could follow the bunny.

"Now you take rabbits," he said. "They love making babies."

Looking her way he chuckled. She looked away and whistled. Her dad whistled all the time. She did not want to take a walk with this man but neither did she dare run away.

"And dogs; they are the most comical. Sometimes the male gets stuck inside the bitch. Funny as hell."

The only way across the creek at the top of the hill was to step carefully from boulder to boulder.

"I caught pollywogs here last spring," she said

"Here we go," Uncle Harry said, scooping her up in his arms and crossing the creek on rough boulders. When they got to the other side, he slid his hand inside her shorts before putting her down. She felt a sensation like a jolt from the electric fence shoot through her body.

"You've got on panties," her uncle said. "How can we swoon if you have on panties?" Swoon? What did swoon mean? She squirmed to get free and he put her down.

Frightened, and feeling sick, she ran across the top of the dam, intending to scramble up the hill on the other side of the pond and run to the house. Who did he think he was, putting his hand inside her shorts? Must be that was what the boys meant when they said they wanted to get into a girls' panties. Feeling awfully scared she bolted up the hill away from the pond.

"Stop running, Phyllis," her uncle demanded. She turned around and saw him standing by the pond peeing into the water. She looked toward the ground and then at the sky where a hawk was circling.

"Come here," he said, "I've got something to show you." He seemed to be holding something and Phyllis thought he had found a four-leaf clover. He eased down to the ground, sitting in soft grasses. She walked to where he sat and he grabbed her arm pulling her down.

"What do you want to show me," she asked innocently.

"This," he said, grabbing her hand and pushing it inside the front opening of his shorts. "There," he said in a satisfied tone. "Isn't that nice." He moved her hand around inside his shorts, pushing it down on his big, hard peter. He put his hand inside her panties rubbing gently. "Ahh. Doesn't that feel good?" Phyllis thought about the bull with heifers when they bred, and wondered in terror what was next. She felt trapped but didn't dare move. He kept using her hand to rub himself, and she thought about how dirty it was. Her mother had been very clear that girls should never let boys touch their breasts or between their legs. Intimacy must be saved for marriage, she said. Her mother would be furious that she

let him touch her private parts. Thinking about how
wrong it was, she snatched her hand away and slid
quickly backward on the grass pushing with her heels,
crushing peppermint plants as she slid away from the
nasty man. The mint plants smelled like chewing gum.

"All right! God damn it." He yelled pushing himself
to his feet. "What the hell is the matter with you?"
Phyllis stood up brushing pieces of grass and peppermint
plants off her shorts as her uncle dashed up the hill toward
the grove. He waited at the top motioning for her to
follow. She wanted to run the other way back down the
pasture path but she didn't dare. He looked angry.
Bending toward her when she caught up with him he
shook his finger in her face.

"Now you listen to me young lady. Your mother and
father wouldn't understand what happened." He had a
sneer on his face that reminded Phyllis of bad guys in
comic books. "They'd say it was dirty," he admonished,
insinuating that his niece had done something wrong.
"Don't you ever forget this is our secret."

He turned and walked briskly down the hill, Phyllis
following him. She heard a rustling in the hedge and
Bowser ran up to her "Good boy," she said touching his
soft head. He looked up at his girl with soft brown eyes
before running on ahead, sniffing the ground as he ran.

At the house, Levina bustled around the kitchen in her
usual no-nonsense way, completely oblivious to her
daughter's feelings.

"Did you have fun at the creek?" Levina asked.

"We walked to the pond," was all she said.

Uncle Harry need not have worried about Phyllis
giving away "their secret." She had no intention of telling
anyone except maybe Betty about what happened in the
woods. What could she say?   She doubted her mother
would believe her. She had a hard time believing it
herself. Levina would think it was another one of her

stories. She knew Uncle Harry would angrily deny it, so she kept quiet just as he had demanded.

Erwin looked up from his newspaper.

"Harry, wait 'til you see this new style bathing suit. You'll love it."

The skimpy two-piece suit called a Bikini was all the rage. It was named in honor of the underwater testing of an atomic bomb near Bikini Atoll in the central Pacific.

Levina pulled a batch of huckleberry muffins out of the oven--Phyllis's favorite. The family sat down to supper of chicken, boiled potatoes, and fresh green beans. Erwin talked about President Truman, saying he would be happy when the Democrats were out of office. Harry Truman became president in 1945 after President Roosevelt died in office.

"Tom Dewey is my choice," Erwin said, speaking of New York State's Republican governor. Levina refilled tea cups. Uncle Harry kept his eyes on his plate as he ate and did not comment on the Bikini, the food or the president.

There was one muffin left on the plate when Uncle Harry reached for it. Phyllis wanted it too, and she glanced at her mother in disappointment. Harry caught the look and quickly scraped his chair across the linoleum covered floor away from the table.

"You miserable, selfish, brat. So you want the last muffin do you?" He threw the muffin at her and stomped out of the room.

Erwin shook his head, picked up a toothpick the way he always did after a meal, and moved to the rocking chair by the window to finish reading the newspaper. Levina stood up, smoothed her apron with her hands, cleared her throat a couple of times, and carried dirty dishes to the sink to be washed. Phyllis picked up Baby Face, her gray and white cat, from under the table and held the kitty in her lap. He purred as she stroked his soft fur.

"Phyllis, please dry the dishes," Levina said as she washed.

No one said a word when Harry hurried through the kitchen carrying his suitcase, mumbling something about a spoiled brat. He left without saying goodbye. The screen door slammed behind him like an exclamation point. Levina cleared her throat again and stacked dishes in the cupboard.

"Good bye," Erwin said without looking up from the paper. Phyllis heard the crunching of tires on the gravel driveway as Uncle Harry drove to the road. She thanked God in a silent prayer that he was gone.

"His damn temper sure hasn't improved with age," Erwin said aloud to no one in particular. And that was the end of it.

It would be another eight years before Phyllis got up the nerve to tell her mother about the bad things that happened on that spoiled summer day when she was ten.

Nine - 1946 Part Two

Erwin, Jay and the Outhouse

Levina was insistent she could not take care of a new baby without indoor plumbing. Phyllis moved to an upstairs bedroom freeing up the small downstairs bedroom. She was almost as excited about having a bathroom again as she was about having a brother, although she secretly hoped the baby would be a sister.

"Erwin, I simply cannot do this without a bathroom." Being ignored was exasperating. Levina's patience was unraveling. Erwin finished up his breakfast coffee, pushed back the chair, and reached for his cap.

"Poor old Pop," he said. "Work, work, work is all I know." *Bitch, bitch, bitch, was what he thought.*

Cinder blocks for the cistern were delivered the next morning. Erwin lugged the heavy blocks to the cellar, one by one, mixed up mortar with a hoe in a wooden box and laid up cistern walls in one corner of the cellar. The clean smell of mortar permeated the house.

"It smells good," Phyllis said poking at it with a stick.

"Yup--it sure does," Erwin said slathering mortar on the blocks and fitting them neatly together. The interior was plastered. Now all they needed was rain to fill the cistern with water.

Levina was thankful every day that she had scraped together enough money from teaching to modernize the kitchen. Bright floral linoleum covered the old floor, and a spanking new white kitchen sink and cupboards had replaced the black pump. God was good.

Eaves troughs were installed all around the roof to catch rain water. Phyllis prayed for rain, lots of rain; she even did a rain dance on the back lawn.

"Don't get carried away," Erwin cautioned his exuberant daughter, "we have second cutting down." Second cutting hay was better quality than first cutting, but getting rained on ruined the hay. Persnickety cows didn't like the taste, and milk production took a dive.

Slowly, ever so slowly, the cellar reservoir filled. Levina peered into the open cistern's dark recesses with a flash light looking for the occasional mouse corpse, adding Clorox to the yellowish water for good measure. Old houses had mice. The critters chewed little openings in the walls, scurried around the lath, and sometimes died there. Phyllis listened to them scampering around inside the walls when she was in bed. Everybody had mice. That's what cats were for, and mouse traps. Overpowering dead mouse odor could make a room uninhabitable. And then there was the small dead mouse that Levina found between the sheets at the very bottom of Phyllis's bed.

"Look at this," Levina said holding the dead mouse by his tail. "He must have gotten lost."

"Must be your stinky feet suffocated him," Erwin teased his daughter.

"That's disgusting," Phyllis said. Erwin laughed. Levina took the mouse outside and threw it to a cat that ran away with the prize.

The plumber's truck arrived in mid-August. "Rah, Rah, Sis Boom Bah!" Phyllis cheered, "For health and good cheer, the tub is here!" Phyllis was thrilled about the bathroom. Now she wouldn't be embarrassed when friends came to visit. Betty's family had always had a bathroom. They even had a shower that Phyllis loved.

Rain water became discolored running down cedar shingles, but it was as soft as rose petals. There were two faucets in the kitchen: well water for drinking, cooking, and washing dishes, non-potable cistern water for everything else. Cistern water was piped to the bathroom for baths only. You didn't drink it or brush your teeth with it.

"All right, Philly," Levina announced on the day Phyllis had been waiting for. She hadn't been in a large

133

bath tub since they lived in Chittenango, and she was the first one to bathe in the brand new white tub. Operating within the guidelines of Levina's "Don't Waste the Water Manifesto," she was not allowed to draw much water— the cistern wasn't full enough. Still, it was an improvement over the itsy bitsy porcelain tub she had crammed into since they moved to the farm. Phyllis prayed again for a deluge.

Sitting in the tub with her allotted amount of water, barely enough to cover the bottom, Phyllis studied the reflection of her shapeless, stick figure body in the shiny chrome faucets. She imagined a shapelier body for herself. Slipping away into her private world she imagined a voluptuous Phyllis. That never happened.

"Don't drain the tub," her mother reminded. Levina added boiling water to the tub when Phyllis was done with her bath, and Erwin used the second hand water without a second thought.

Water conservation was a way of life. One shallow well served the house and the barn. The cows had priority. Water was precious. It was rationed, saved, recycled and never, ever wasted. They brushed their teeth with half a glass of water, not under a running faucet, and only flushed the toilet, in Levina's words, "when absolutely necessary." Levina insisted it was not necessary to flush after every tinkle. The garden was watered with recycled water from laundry tubs, dishes, baths, and after washing the milking machines.

Washday was a once-a-week occurrence, usually Monday unless it rained. Water was heated in a big metal container called a boiler on the coal stove in the winter and on a kerosene stove in the summer. The washing machine was supported by four legs with wheels. It was used in the wood shed, a kind of mud room, for warm-weather washing, and wheeled into the kitchen in cold weather. Two galvanized metal rinse tubs were set up next to the rotund washing machine.

The weekly wash took all day using the agitating washer with two rubber wringers. Piles of soiled laundry with a locker room odor covered the floor. Wash water was used over and over working from least dirty to most dirty laundry. Homemade lye soap was grated into the groaning washing machine. Levina added a gallon-size tea kettle full of boiling water and Clorox each time she started a new load.

Feeding items through rubber wringers was dangerous business. Levina's friend Minnie had leaned over too far earlier in the year, and one of her breasts got caught in the wringers along with a bath towel.

"Her breast was black and blue. Thank the Lord she was able to reach the controls to stop the machine before more damage was done," Levina told Phyllis repeatedly so she wouldn't forget. She fed sheets, pillow cases and towels through the cylindrical wringers from the washing machine into two galvanized tubs of rinse water, one after the other, as she talked. Phyllis could only hope she would eventually have breasts large enough to get caught in anything.

Clothesline stretched across the back lawn from the house to trees and back again. Laundry ruffling in hill-top breezes formed a grand, pulsating washday parade and perfumed the house when baskets of dry clothes were brought inside. There was nothing more refreshing than clean, line-dried sheets and pillow cases. In the winter wet laundry froze stiff; Erwin's dungarees stood up by themselves. The laundry was brought inside and draped on big wooden laundry racks to finish drying.

Phyllis imagined the billowing, flapping sheets were sails on clipper ships heading to the Spice Islands, although she had no idea where or what the Spice Islands were.

"I'm riding to the store," Phyllis said as she walked out of the house after lunch on a sunny summer day.

"Watch out for the trucks," Levina cautioned. Massive dump trucks loaded with crushed rock and stone dust roared down the road back and forth to Worlock Stone Quarry all day long going a mile a minute leaving road kill in their wake.

Being ten years old and having her very own bike was the best thing in the world. Phyllis rolled her sleek red and white bicycle out of the tool shed running her hands over the smooth chrome handle bars.

"Thanks again, Grandpa," she whispered. She coasted out of the rough driveway, looking both ways before pedaling hard down the road past Rosie's house. She needed to get a good start in order to make it up Jay's hill.

Maybe she would meet other kids at the general store. Then they would cruise up and down the road through Perryville, and ride to Perryville Falls. She had a nickel in her pocket for a Dixie Cup from her jelly jar piggy bank.

"I hope David is there," she whispered, "I hope, I hope." If he showed up, he would ride with her back to the farm. That day no one showed up. *"Boring,"* Phyllis thought.

Slipping unnoticed through the tattered screen door into the store, she headed to the dusty, ice cream freezer in the back of the building. The freezer made a steady hum. She collected pictures of movie stars that were printed on the inside of round cardboard Dixie Cup tops. Standing by the freezer trying to decide between chocolate and vanilla or strawberry and vanilla ice cream, (those were the only choices) she heard the door slam and recognized their neighbor Jay's gruff voice.

Jay was a grungy, tobacco-chewing, cussing, clowning old guy who lived with his ancient mother on a dilapidated little farm on the opposite side of the road not far from the Lambert's. Phyllis's mom said he was a disgrace. His clothes smelled like the cow barn, his hair was long and scraggly, he cursed, and chewed tobacco. It was his bad language that bothered Phyllis's mom the most. He took the Lord's name in vain and talked dirty. Phyllis sometimes used one or two of Jay's dirty words, but not if her mother was around. Jay's hair curled around his touring cap and, as always, he held a cud of tobacco in his cheek.

"You can smell Jay a mile away," Levina often said, and that day was no exception. Jay did not bother to change his clothes and boots when he went away. He reeked of cow manure. Jay was leaning over the counter towards Frank, the proprietor, like he had a story to tell. He loved telling stories. Frank was looking down, counting money and IOU's and quite obviously leaning upwind from his malodorous customer.

Holding a vanilla and strawberry Dixie Cup, Phyllis moved closer to the counter to pay for the ice cream. Jay's back was toward her and he did not see her waiting.

"Wanna hear a good one?" Jay asked. Frank did not answer but Jay started talking anyway.

"I moseyed up ta the Lambert's t'other day like I do ta pass the time. Lambert, Lummie we call him, says he needs help with a little project."

Jay removed his cap, scratched his balding head, and spat a dark stream of tobacco juice into a large tin can that stood on the floor by the counter especially for such purpose.

"Lummie says his ole lady is naggin' him ta move the privy. She figured now that they've got their indoor toilet it's time to move the two-holer further away from the house." Jay took off his cap again for another spit and wiped his bushy mustache on his sleeve. "Lummie said the little woman; he calls her Ma, had a conniption fit that morning about the smell of the Crapper when the wind was blowing from that direction. "

'Today is the day,' she said. T'weren't the first time she'd asked. Lambert had the 1020 hooked up ta the stone-boat and was trying ta figure out what ta do next."

"I say their privy don't smell near as bad as most. Then I notice the ole lady standin' on the back stoop all official like with her hands on her hips. I motion ta Lummie with my head but he knows she's watching. He says the Dutch are known for their fas-tid-i-ous-ness. I notice he turns t'other way so she don't see him winkin' and grinnin'. You know Lummie, always singin' and whistlin' and likin' a good joke. But his ole lady has a real serious way of lookin' at sit-she-ations. "

"So we get to work pushin' and jostlin' the privy a piece with lots of gruntin' and grumblin' and cussin' to get it off the top of the old pit and onto the sledge. Lummie says we'll fill in the hole later. Then the old lady comes runnin' over with her Brownie like she's documentin' a big event. Lummie, he lights up a Camel and we stand next to the privy. Then I say nice and loud so the ole lady is sure ta hear me, **'Just two shits movin' a shit house.'** She don't much like my language but Lummie laughs like hell. Ya should'a seen her face, red as a beet. She hustled back to the house real disgusted like sayin' she wishes I would not use THAT word. Lummie and me, we get back ta work pullin' the outhouse 'roun' behind the toolshed like she wants it. We gets it all sit-she-ated over the pit and Lummie says maybe we should initiate the new location. I say, hell no. Sure as hell as I unbutton my pants she'll show up to take another picture."

Jay laughed real loud, removed his hat and took another long spit.

"If that's the best story you can come up with, you should've stayed home," Frank said without looking up.

He was still counting IOU receipts from the big, silver cash register. Jay removed his hat, scratched his head again and laughed at his own story.

Jay had stopped yakking so Phyllis stepped up to the counter to pay for the ice cream. Jay was startled by the sight of the little girl and got a worried look. Phyllis knew from experience how much her mom hated THAT word and Jay knew from her grin that she had heard the story.

"Hey, Cricket," Jay said using the nickname he had given her because of her long legs. "Ya ain't gonna tell your Ma I was talking about her are ya?" Phyllis shook her head back and forth. Jay's grin displayed tobacco-stained teeth. He took a nickel out of his pocket and paid for her ice cream.

Phyllis thanked Jay and opened the Dixie Cup. They had a deal.

The State Fair was the best place to celebrate the end of the summer, but Levina was pregnant, and had no intention of traipsing around the fair grounds. Erwin went for a day with his friend, Clate, and would have taken Phyllis had Levina not objected.

"I need you to collect eggs. We'll go to Chittenango later," her mother promised, "and don't forget the oyster shells."

"Shit," Phyllis said out loud when she was alone in the barn. It was definitely an appropriate time for THAT word. Erwin's hip-roofed barn was connected to a smaller shed, an afterthought Levina called it. The addition connecting the barn to the chicken house, had a wide wooden plank floor where a hay wagon could be pulled in out of the weather. Four steps down on the far side led to the hen house door.

As usual, she prayed that the vicious rooster who strutted around like he owned the place wasn't there. He enjoyed attacking little girls. She heard him crowing outside and knew the coast was clear. Reaching under hens in the nests, she cradled the warm eggs, carefully placing them in a worn wicker basket, and made her getaway back across the dusty, feather-strewn dirt floor to safety.

She eased down in a pile of hay on the plank floor of the addition where Bowser was waiting. The old dog plunked down next to her with his head on her lap.

"You are my absolute best buddy," she said, smoothing the soft fur around his ears.

A year earlier, Phyllis's father, Erwin, had hired two men to catch droves of rabbits who lived under the plank floor. The invasion had started simply enough. Someone gave Phyllis a pair of pet rabbits. Somehow they got out of their pen and, as rabbits will, they began raising families—one family after the other under the plank floor. The rabbit round-up was funny until one of the rabbit wranglers said he was chasing his rabbit stew. Phyllis tried not to think about it. Her family did not eat rabbit.

"Uncle Harry was right about rabbits," she whispered to Bowser. She couldn't get that summer afternoon out of her mind when her uncle asked her to show him the pond. She considered telling her mother the story, but, once again thought better of it. Levina said she had an imagination that worked overtime and would probably think Phyllis had made it up.

"Life isn't fair," she said to Bowser. "Darn, darn, darn." She really wanted to go to the fair.

Duty interrupted reverie when she heard her mother call her name. She got up reluctantly, grabbed the basket by the handle and carried the eggs to the house with Bowser at her heels. In the kitchen she wiped the eggs clean with a damp dish rag and weighed each one. The egg scale registered small, medium, large or extra-large.

Phyllis arranged the brown eggs by size in baskets, being careful not to crack the shells. They could not sell cracked eggs. Levina sold her eggs to Tiffany's grocery store in Chittenango, and used her egg money to buy groceries. She rarely shopped at the Red and White Perryville store. It was too expensive, and not the cleanest place in the world.

Phyllis stood by the window watching for the big yellow bus on the first Monday after Labor Day when Erwin came in whistling from the barn as though he didn't have a care in the world. She was nervous about transferring to the central school in Cazenovia. Perryville classes ended after fourth grade.

The breakfast table was set and coffee simmered on the stove. Bowser squeezed in behind Erwin and Phyllis reached to pet him as Erwin lifted the large, galvanized milk pail containing fresh milk, to the kitchen counter. Warm milk sloshed against the side of the pail in frothy waves, just inches from Phyllis's nose—a sickening smell in her estimation. She pinched her nose shut.

"What kind of a farmer's daughter are you," her father teased, "not liking milk?" Erwin drank a tall glass of cold milk every day with a contented "ahhhhh." Phyllis poured Hershey's chocolate syrup into the glass that she was forced to drink for supper every single night. They drank it unpasteurized without any hesitation. Erwin kept a healthy herd.

Bowser had taken her attention, and when she glanced back through the window, the bus was at the corner above the house. She wanted to say "damn," but in Levina's presence cussing was modified. "Darn!" Phyllis grabbed her lunch box and her book bag, and dashed for the door.

"Study hard, Babe," Erwin chortled. "Get a hundred in everything."

"Be careful; don't fall," Levina cautioned, wearing a worried expression. Levina never stopped worrying that Phyllis, with her tender skin, would hurt herself, which she often did, and had the scars to prove it. She dashed down the driveway, crossed the road and stood on the shoulder next to the large, rectangular metal mailbox that was attached to a fence post stuck in an old milk can full of gravel. The snow plow had rammed it several times last winter, and according to Levina, it looked like a war horse. Brakes squealed, the bus stopped and the door opened. Levina waved from the front window, but Phyllis didn't see her. Levina was home because she had given up her teaching job joking that she was having a $5,000 baby. She had just signed her contract for the 1946-47 school-year when she found out she was pregnant.

"*Shit*," Phyllis thought. Her mother did not like to hear that word, but she could think the word as much as she wanted to. "*Shit*." Aunt Gladys, Erwin's younger sister whom Phyllis really liked, used the word regularly much to Levina's consternation. Whenever her daughter slipped and said "shit" out loud, Levina accused her of being just like her Aunt Gladys. That was fine with Phyllis.

Phyllis studied the floor as she entered the grungy bus and eased into the first vacant seat without speaking to anyone. She sat down without looking around because she was saving a seat for Betty who lived a mile up the hill in Fenner Township. Phyllis and Betty had met in church, shyly peeking at each other over the pews. They were Sunday school buddies before they were best friends.

Phyllis felt very lucky having Betty for a best friend. She was pretty, thoughtful, and very popular. Lots of kids wanted to be her friend. A sprightly redhead, she had attended school in Cazenovia since kindergarten because her father's prosperous farm was outside the Perryville School district Although she was a farmer's daughter, she was accepted by the townies. Phyllis would soon learn that Perryville School transfers were dubbed "farmers" by town kids.

Phyllis stared through the window as the driver shifted gears and the bus inched slowly up the hill past Jay's ramshackle little farm. She imagined his old mother inside the dirty, cluttered house making lace curtains. She smiled, thinking about Jay treating her to ice cream in return for her silence about the back-house story. The bus stopped at Perryville School where the younger kids got off. No one else sat in the seat next to her, and it was vacant a few stops later when Betty bounced up the steps and skipped down the aisle.

"I wonder which class we'll be in," Betty mused.

Phyllis had not realized there was more than one class. She followed Betty when they got off the bus in Cazenovia worried that if she lost sight of her friend she would get lost. The Central School was huge compared to Perryville. The building had a strange smell. Many odors competed for attention: green sweeping compound that janitors threw on the floors before pushing brooms down the halls, body odor from myriad students crushed together in the halls, the sweet fragrance of pretty, young female teachers wearing an over-abundance of perfume, the haze of tobacco smoke whenever the Teachers' Room door opened, food from the cafeteria, chalk dust, Ditto fluid on duplicated purple pages teachers handed out (and that kids liked to sniff) and sawdust from the wood shop. Boys took shop and girls took homemaking in Junior High, and never the other way around. Fresh coats of wax on the shiny hall floors were already getting scuffed up.

There were two fifth grade sections. Phyllis and Betty were assigned to different rooms. She doesn't remember whether there were Perryville kids in her section. Mrs. Middleton, the teacher, welcomed students with the usual assignment—to write about their summer experiences. She was not completely honest about it.

Phyllis and David sat next to each other in the large social hall on the second floor of the school building, waiting for the movie to begin. The Methodist church sponsored community pot luck suppers one Friday night a month at the school. The best part was the movie the pastor showed after the meal.

"Why is your mother wearing a smock?" David asked.

"She's having a baby." David looked surprised.

"We got a bathroom.

"You didn't have a bathroom?"

"We did before we moved, then we didn't. Now we do."

"Do you like fifth grade?" David was a year younger and still attended Perryville School.

"No. The brat town kids are mean. They call us farmers."

"So what! You are a farmer."

David was not a farmer. He did not understand how it felt to be called one while mean kids held their noses. Some of the bullies called Phyllis horse face and phyl-lice but she didn't mention that. David lived with his parents and little sister just down the main drag from the school. His father worked in an office.

After dinner, the women cleared the tables and packed away leftovers. Kids ran around screeching and dashing up and down stairs to the anteroom where the bathrooms were located and then stomped back upstairs playing tag.

People got as comfortable as they could in straight back wooden chairs, cleared their throats, chatted and laughed as the minister fumbled with the reel-to-reel movie projector. Kids sat in the back rows. The film broke and it took a few minutes to splice it back together. When the film was threaded from one reel to another, the projector sputtered into action. Dust motes danced in the bright beam of light, and random numbers appeared upside down on the screen.

Someone switched off the lights. David reached for Phyllis's hand. Music blared as the movie, "The Enchanted Forest," began.

"I want to write movie stories when I grow up," Phyllis whispered.

A massive black steam locomotive pulling a train of Pullman sleeper cars roared into view. The engine careened down a steep hill on tracks that clung to a narrow ridge along the river. A violent rain storm whipped through the forest bending tall pine trees as the huge steam engine hurtled around a sharp curve. Phyllis grabbed the side of her chair. Lightning flashed, thunder crashed and brakes on metal wheels squealed. The last Pullman car and the caboose jumped the track and careened down a rocky incline toward the river as the rest of the train disappeared down the track.

A baby screamed. Phyllis's hand tightened on David's. The crying continued. In the confusion, Old John, a hermit who lived in a hollowed out Red Wood tree, found the baby boy who was thrown from the train in his basket. Old John rescued the boy and raised him in the Enchanted Forest until the special day many years later when he was reclaimed by his parents.

"Wow," what a good movie," Phyllis said.

"Yup," David said, "it was good."

A babble of voices and laughter filled the room as David brushed Phyllis's cheek with a kiss. Her face felt warm, and she touched the place on her cheek where she could still feel the touch of his lips.

Ten – 1947

"Wake up Babe," Erwin said rousing his daughter who was asleep on the studio couch in the family room. "I've got to take Ma to the hospital."

Phyllis & Donna

Levina sat on a kitchen chair wearing her old winter coat. A suitcase was next to the chair. Bleary-eyed, Phyllis put her coat on over her pajamas, pulled the hood up, and slipped into her boots. Her breath froze instantly; and floated like a cloud in the frigid winter night air. Erwin turned the key, but the old car made a grinding noise, refusing to start.

He adjusted the choke, turned the key again and the engine sputtered to life.

"Poor old buggy doesn't like this damn cold weather any better than I do," Erwin complained.

Phyllis shivered. She wanted to get back in bed, cuddling under the covers.

"It's bone chilling," Levina said with a sigh of resignation, stretching her long, wool coat around her bulging belly, "but it is only February."

When others complained about long winters, Levina said she didn't mind the cold, because: *"If we had no winter, the spring would not be so pleasant."* *(Anne Bradstreet).*

A faint light glowed in their neighbor's kitchen when Erwin drove into the driveway at the top of Hart's Hill. Bob and Iva would be asleep but they were expecting her at any time. The kitchen door inside the enclosed porch would be unlocked. No one locked their doors.

"Thank the Lord it isn't snowing," Levina whispered as Phyllis got out of the car and walked toward the door. "Be a good girl."

Phyllis wondered how she could be anything but good. She was going right to bed in the small bedroom located off the kitchen. Her dream of having a sibling was coming true, but she was so tired all she could think of was getting back to bed.

Erwin turned the car around and headed back down the hill for the 35-mile drive to Syracuse with his pregnant wife. Levina's friend, Julia, would meet them at the hospital. Erwin had to be home for morning chores.

"Isn't that the hell of it," Erwin grumbled when Julia phoned the following afternoon saying he had another daughter. "You've got a sister," Erwin said matter-of-factly, "yup, another girl."

Erwin was obviously disgruntled about not getting their John Rodney. Phyllis had wanted a sister all along. Boy or no boy, Erwin placed a box of cigars on the counter at Perryville store in honor of the newest little Lambert. It was tradition. Phyllis was so happy she could hardly stand it. She wrote a letter to her mother and sister that Erwin took to the hospital.

Dear Mom,

Dad went down too (sic) Chittenango and I was here alone but Bowser was in here with me. Dad came home and got the mail. I was very pleased with your nice letter. I had a letter form (sic) Aunt Marie. I can hardly read her writing. Daddy had a piece off (sic) limberger (sic) cheese. Whew. He told me to be a good sport so I ate with him.

Daddy had not made the bed since you left so I made it. I also washed the dishes. Yesterday Daddy washed and moped the floor. We got the life (sic) magazine. Daddy will bring it up for you. It has the picture of Grace Moore before and after she was killed.

I hope we can get up Sunday. But right now it is storming quite hard. This morning I cleaned Dickey (canary) up but I did not give him a bath.

I'm anxious to see Donna. Golly can hardly wait. I am trying to keep the house clean. Betwine (sic) Daddy and me were (sic) managing quite well.

I had a good music lesson and Daddy came down after me. Nina asked me how you were. I miss you an awful lot so does Daddy and Bowser.

We had our baton picture. I wore my long sleeve blouse and plain skirt. I wish I could come to the Hospitle (sic) and see you and donna (sic) I still do my chores out to the barn and take Bowser out every night.

With much love
Phyllis

A week later, Phyllis tacked a WELCOME HOME sign on the door, and had dinner planned for the home coming. She had learned to cook and clean at an early age.

"You'll make some lucky man a good wife, Babe," Erwin said admiring the clean farm house.

The baby girl was named Donna Marie, (Donna after their minister, Rev. Peckam's wife, and Marie after Levina's sister).

Levina nervously checked her daughter's skin every day. There was no sign that Donna had inherited the family skin condition, and for that Levina gave thanks.

Phyllis dashed outside when Erwin drove in the yard with Levina and Donna. Running to the car, she saw a chubby little girl wrapped in a pink blanket. Donna was perfection in her sister's estimation. Her thick, dark hair was almost long enough to braid. Gazing at the little cherub, Phyllis wondered how she could love her so much when she had just seen her for the first time.

Winter's long season sped up for Phyllis that year taking care of her very own sister. She cooed and fussed and giggled, delighted as she could be that she was no longer an only child. A built-in babysitter, she had baby duty the minute she got home from school.

"Change your clothes and wash your hands before you pick up the baby," Levina reminded her daily.

"Be careful to support her head, keep her covered with a blanket, and burp her after every ounce." *"I know, I know,"* Phyllis thought. *"I'm not stupid."*

Diaper changing was easy. Phyllis practiced on a doll until she was ready for the challenge. She wiped Donna's little bottom, sprinkled baby powder in a fragrant cloud, rinsed out the diaper and put it in the white enamel diaper pail to soak in a solution of water and 20 Mule

Team Borax. She held a finger between Donna's little thighs and the cotton cloth diaper when pinning. There were no disposable diapers in the Lambert home.

Phyllis cuddled her baby sister in the kitchen rocking chair, keeping time to the bobbing lid of the big aluminum tea kettle on the stove as they rocked. Levina washed the supper dishes, scooping warm water out of the reservoir that was built into the stove. She was fanatical about rinsing the dishes with boiling water out of the kettle. A radio soap opera drama played out, forming pictures in Phyllis's mind of a romantic love affair gone awry.

Phyllis coaxed a bottle of warm Similac formula into Donna's rosebud mouth and laughed at how eagerly she sucked the nipple. When formula dribbled down her little chin, Phyllis wiped it with a clean diaper and hoisted the baby up to her shoulder, patting gently on her little back until she burped. *Gosh this is fun*, she thought. Having a sister was the best thing in the world.

Winter passed in a blur. Donna grew much faster than Phyllis expected. Big sister stayed in the house more and went to the barn less. Erwin reckoned he had lost his hired hand. He got up with the fussy baby every night saying that Ma needed her rest.

Phyllis slept downstairs on the studio couch for the winter, reveling in her dad's lullaby, "Ahh, ahh ahh, my lambie, ahh, ahh, ahh my low."

She often pondered when she woke up during the night, trying to imagine what her life was like when she was a baby. Had her father sung to her? All she knew was what she had been told and what she read in her baby book.

She thought about her dad who she adored, remembering one night in particular soon after she and Levina had moved to Perryville. She was in bed in the small upstairs bedroom when her father came up to say good night.

"Give your old dad a kiss," he said leaning over the bed.

Phyllis felt shy around her father, and turning her face to the wall, she pretended not to hear. There was a strong smell of creosote from an old chimney that ran through the room. She stared at the faded floral wall paper around the chimney that was stained brown sensing her father standing by her bed waiting for the kiss. Soon he walked out of the room and didn't ask again. That was all she remembered about it with no good reason to explain her actions. She was sorry, but it would be many years before she got up the nerve to finally give her dad the kiss he wanted.

March was predictably chilly. Erwin tapped five sugar maples in the front yard and the big maple in the back yard by pounding metal spouts into the trunks. "Ouch," Phyllis yelped, wondering if the trees grimaced in pain. Rosie said plants had feelings just like humans. There had to be freezing nights and warm days for the sap to run. Phyllis imagined the sap with little legs running up and down tunnels inside the trees.

The Lambert's sugar bush was small but it was plenty big enough to supply the family with delicious maple syrup and extra to give away. Phyllis put on her coat, boots and gloves every morning before school to make the rounds of the sugar maples, pouring sap from small pails that hung on the spouts into a larger collection pail. She did the same thing every afternoon after school.

She poured the sweet, clear liquid that looked like water into one of the large pots that her mother had simmering on the coal-burning kitchen range. As the sap in the finishing pot evaporated, it was transformed into delicious amber colored syrup that Levina sealed hot in quart Mason jars.   The kitchen smelled like a candy factory.

"We don't have much money," Erwin said, sopping up maple syrup with fresh pancakes, "but we sure know how to eat."   He kept a quart jar of sweet cold sap in the refrigerator for drinking.

On April 21, Phyllis and Princess Elizabeth celebrated their mutual birthday.   Phyllis wondered what she would say if by some miracle she got to meet the princess she so admired, the down-to-earth-princess who worked as a truck driver and mechanic during the war.   She kept news stories and pictures of the princess in her scrapbook.

Phyllis carefully removed the wrapping paper on each gift so that it could be used again.   The last gift was a diary with a red leather cover. "My Everyday DIARY" was printed in gold letters on the front.   Calendars for 1934 and 1935 were printed inside the front cover and 1936 and 1937 calendars were on the last page.   Lists of facts and statistics were printed on pages at the back of the journal: a list of U. S. Presidents starting with George Washington and ending with Franklin Delano Roosevelt. Levina said she had kept the journal for a special time. It didn't matter to Phyllis that the diary was older than she was.   When she put her gifts away, she tucked the diary in her desk.

Levina was warming up left-overs for lunch and Phyllis was feeding Donna Gerber's baby cereal when they heard the mailman honk his car horn.   He was in the driveway and that meant they had a package.   Phyllis handed Donna a piece of Zwieback toast to keep her quiet and ran outside to get the package.

"This is bulky, young lady," the mailman said. "I'll carry it inside for you."   He reached in the back seat for a large cardboard box with round holes on the top and sides. Phyllis heard chirping and shuffling sounds and knew it held baby chicks. She felt happy and excited all at the same time.

"Mom, the chicks are here!" she yelled running ahead of the mailman.

"Oh my," Levina said, taking the box from him. She removed the lid and slid it on the floor in back of the kitchen stove as the tiny chicks scrambled for position, peeping disapproval at being jostled.

"Thanks for the coffee and cookies," the mailman said, smiling at Levina.

Levina often left coffee and cookies in the mail box. Erwin said she was buttering up the mailman. Obviously he appreciated her kindness.

Phyllis sat on the floor watching the fluffy yellow birds with big black eyes check out their new home in sideways glances. Levina put a saucer of chicken starter mash (corn meal) and a water container in the box. Baby chicks exude a distinctive spicy smell; it was pleasant having them in the kitchen. Rosie came up to see the chicks after Phyllis phoned.

"Hear that?" Rosie said, listening to the peeping and scrambling and scratching in the box. "That's the music of the earth."

They soon outgrew their snug kitchen nursery, and were moved to the brooder hut, a small building separate from the barn. Early May weather was still cold and a heat lamp hung low from a beam in the center of the building. Phyllis had baby chick duty and was amused by their cute antics, bickering, teasing and competing. When their crops were full they nestled close together under the lamp, maneuvering to get the choice center spot under the lamp, softly chirping at each other. It was the best time of their lives.

When the chicks feathered out and were large enough to know their way around, the door was left open during the day so they could range and gobble up fresh grasses and bugs. That fall the pullets would be integrated with the older hens in the hen house which was not easy. The old-timers resented the young interlopers and they pecked and fussed making life for the new comers as miserable as possible. The young roosters faced a much sadder fate— the freezer. The Lamberts didn't have a deep freezer of their own. They rented a frozen food locker at Lerner's in Canastota and picked up meat whenever they needed it.

By the summer of 1947, Erwin acquired a second-hand Farmall-H tractor with rubber tires. The tractor replaced the horses for many tasks which made life a tad easier, and gave the horses more pasture time. Erwin's life was a paradox: a cheerful man singing and whistling and the man who sometimes struck out in anger. When Phyllis and Levina moved to the farm, Erwin milked by hand a dozen or more cows, twice a day. He was never completely resigned to the life of a dairy farmer. A chicken ranch in California was his dream, and he never quite let go of it.

Erwin sat on the metal milk stool with his capped forehead pressed against the soft flank of the cow he was milking. He milked dry two teats and then two more with a steady stream of milk until it filled the pail. The milk was their bread and butter, their livelihood, and when a cantankerous cow lifted a dirty hoof in protest and tipped over the pail of milk it was a disaster.

"Goddamit!!" Erwin yelled, jumping to his feet.

Phyllis looked up from the kitten she was petting, startled by her father's yell, and saw a pail full of rich, creamy milk streaming across the floor. Cats clamored to lick it up before it disappeared in the manure-spattered gutter. Her father grabbed the oversize barn broom like a club, bringing it down on the unfortunate cow's back bone with a sickening thud. The startled cow bellowed

154

and strained to get out of the stanchion. Erwin might have hit her again, but the first assault split the handle.

Phyllis cried out and tears filled her eyes. She couldn't believe what she had seen. Erwin was still swearing as he dashed to the milk house to wash the pail and begin again. Phyllis felt sick that her father had hurt the poor cow. She would write about it, but she wouldn't tell her mother. She didn't understand pent-up frustration when one was sick and tired of everything. Her father didn't often lose control. Most of the time he seemed very happy, but at other times he swore he would sell the whole damn herd. That spring was one of those times. Saying he was through being tied to the damn old bolognas, Erwin sold the milk cows to George who owned a big farm on the opposite end of Perryville.

Phyllis's herd favorite was a big white cow with an unshapely knee named Pet. The cow and the girl both had problems with their knees swelling up, and they sometimes had discussions about their maladies.

George and his hired men showed up at Erwin's barn saying they were having a round up. Every cow except Pet walked along following the leader, but the big white cow stood in the driveway refusing to move while Phyllis hung on to her neck.

"Get in the house," Erwin ordered.

"I don't want her to leave!" Phyllis cried.

"We don't always get what we want," her father yelled, "now get in the house like you were told."

When Phyllis was out of sight, Pet shuffled along following the other cows. The men drove the herd onto the road and urged them along in single file on the shoulder of the highway to their new home on the other side of the village.

Phyllis rode her bike up the road every week to George's pasture to visit Pet. The cow walked to the fence where they talked about the old days. When cold weather arrived, all the cows disappeared inside the barn. By that time Erwin had bought a new herd, one at a time at auctions, saying he was a damn fool.

The arrival of the Farmall put Phyllis out of a job. She missed her teamster's job a lot. Levina drove the tractor and Phyllis babysat. Erwin said the horses did not mind being put out to pasture part time. He still found uses for them, in his words, "to earn their oats." They pulled the manure sleigh through snow where the tractor got bogged down; they were trained to stop and go, pulling the stone boat while Erwin loaded ubiquitous rocks unearthed by the plow before cultivating new crops; they pulled the manure spreader and he hitched them up to the hay wagon when he picked up scatterings. Silver, who Phyllis loved the most, had a beautiful blond mane and tail. They were not a fancy breed like Clydesdale, Belgian, Draft or Percheron, but to Phyllis they were the best team of work horses in the world.

Jay, the farrier, was a burly man who drove a huge sedan loaded with a trunk full of blacksmith tools. He had a shock of graying hair under his fedora and wore a leather apron. Phyllis ran from the house when she heard his car roar up the drive, anxious for the show to begin. She liked being in the middle of the action.

Jay crouched and held one huge hoof at a time in his lap, smoothing and filing the pungent hooves that smelled like dirty sneakers. Bowser ran off with pieces of hoof in his mouth, chewing them like bones. Jay put the hoof down on the barn floor, adjusted an unlit cigar that he clenched in his teeth, pounded the steel shoe noisily on an anvil to the right size, lifted the hoof again, bent the huge leg at the knee and nailed a steel horse shoe directly to the hoof.

"It doesn't hurt," he'd grin, noticing Phyllis wince, "no more than cutting your toe nails."

Phyllis didn't have toenails like normal people because of the inherited family condition. Instead of being smooth, they were shaped like ugly kernels of corn. She didn't tell Jay because he would think she was weird. She tried to hide the truth about her toe nails by always wearing shoes. She donned a pair of rubber shoes when she went swimming. The kids at Camp Casowasco kidded her about her ugly rubber shoes. She was envious of her friends' smooth toe nails that they polished bright red.

"He's a handsome brute, but he's unfaithful to his wife," Levina said as Jay drove away, "and Jennie is such a nice woman." Jennie did wall papering for Levina.

Phyllis examined a shiny flat-headed horseshoe nail she had picked up off the barn floor. She didn't care whether or not Jay was faithful; she was thinking about her funny looking corn-kernel toenails. She hated having the blasted skin disease

Phyllis took to her big-sister role with exuberance. There were not any complaints about babysitting her sister that first summer. Phyllis dressed Donna like a doll in pretty little gift dresses, whereas Levina usually didn't bother to dress her up. During hay days Phyllis watched Donna until a load of hay arrived at the barn. Erwin packed the load of hay while Levina drove the new tractor.

Levina put Donna in her wooden playpen that was set up on the lawn, and Phyllis switched from baby sitter to farmhand, helping unload the hay. She was very good at setting the big hay fork that hoisted the hay into the mow, and pulling the trip rope to dump the load when her father yelled "stop" from the mow. Levina drove the 1020 that through a series of ropes and pulleys pulled the huge fork full of hay into the barn. (They could not use the 1020 tractor in the fields because the cleated steel wheels dug up the ground and the crops).

"Why can't I have a pony? I'll take care of him," Phyllis pleaded between bites of pie. It was an oft-repeated mantra. Some of her friends had riding horses. She knew how to ride.

"Good pie, Ma." Erwin said sipping his coffee.

"We'll see," Levina said.

Phyllis crossed her arms and pouted. "Other kids have ponies. Why can't I?"

"I said we'll see," Levina iterated.

Phyllis and Donna were sitting on a blanket on the lawn the afternoon a truck with high wooden sides bounced up the driveway with a small, brown pony on board. Brown Pony was not particularly interested in getting off the truck. Phyllis was disappointed the minute she saw her She was not what she had pictured in her mind. She wanted her pony to have a longer, lighter color mane and tail like Roy Roger's horse Trigger.

"She's got mean eyes," Levina said.

Phyllis saddled her, sat on her, dismounted and repeated the procedure many times over the next few weeks. Nothing changed. Brown Pony was more stubborn than a mule. The rider was petrified. Annie Oakley, or whoever she was on a particular day, coaxed and pleaded with Brown Pony. Now and then, they made it to the field behind the barn before she bolted and dashed back to the barn door where she resumed her resolute stance.

"What the heck are you doing?" Erwin asked. "Don't just sit there. Ride. She needs exercise." Phyllis had rehearsed her excuses. That day she was a general in the Union Army. They were resting after a battle. She was talking to her men

"Bullshit," said Erwin. "Show her who's boss." Erwin swatted the animal's rump. Brown Pony jumped but she did not move far. It was time, Erwin decided, to show Phyllis a thing or two about horses. The pony owner's father had barely swung his leg over the pony's back when the lethargic animal had a sudden burst of bucking bronco energy. Erwin was barely seated in the western saddle when Brown Pony raised her hind legs and ejected Erwin over her head onto the hard-packed dirt driveway. The pony owner's father struggled back to his feet and dusted himself off. The resulting diatribe wasn't pretty; something about a "miserable, useless son-of-a-bitch who wasn't worth her weight in salt."

A few days later the dented brown truck that delivered Brown Pony returned to retrieve the problem animal. Phyllis was just coming out of the barn and could not make her getaway in time.

The truck driver hung out his window and yelled, "Hey kid, why don't you want your pony?" The easiest thing to do was cry and run, and that is what she did. There was no further pony talk in the Lambert household.

Aunt Marie had a flair for interior design. She had transformed a square doorway between her living room and dining room into an arch and beamed with pride at her accomplishment. After showing off her architectural achievement to her visiting sister, she made a big fuss over Donna. That was the day Phyllis made an exciting discovery.

Kenny was a teenager, five and one-half years older than Phyllis and fifteen months older than his brother Jerry. Phyllis envied them because they got to sleep all summer in an army surplus tent that was pitched under trees in the front yard. They also hung khaki-colored hammocks in the trees that zipped up to keep out mosquitoes. Phyllis thought boys had all the fun.

159

The boys weren't around that day. She assumed they were somewhere in the barn tinkering on an old motor, because that was what they loved to do. Tinkering on engines was hazardous to their tender skin and their fingers were permanently wrapped in bandages that Aunt Marie made from ripping up old sheets. They had lost nearly all their fingernails. Kenny and Jerry smelled of axle grease and salve.

Phyllis had not intended to snoop; she just wanted to see the tent. She thought the pile of magazines under one of the army cots was a stack of comic books, but her eyes grew two sizes larger when she saw the pictures. People of all ages, shapes and sizes, whole families, were standing around totally naked. A few of the women had on shorts but otherwise nothing was concealed. By the casual looks on their faces they were unconcerned about being naked as they went about their business. Wide-eyed, she flipped the pages quickly, eager to see as many naked bodies as possible. She had not realized there were such places as nudist colonies.

Totally engrossed, she didn't hear her mother calling her name until Levina got close to the tent. Phyllis tucked one of the nudist colony magazines under her shirt and left the tent trying to act as innocent as she was when she went in.

"It's time to go." Levina had Donna in her arms and Aunt Marie walked them to the car, handing Phyllis a fresh loaf of fragrant bread. Donna shrieked in delight at a slew of new kittens tumbling along behind them.

"More darn kittens." Aunt Marie was not pleased. She used the paper bag and pail of water solution for feline population explosions. Donna would intercede a few years later talking her pragmatic aunt into a stay of execution for an adorable gray tiger kitten with eyes as big as saucers. He lived a long and happy life as Tommy Lambert, house cat.

The magazine remained Phyllis's secret until she showed it to her friends, Mary and Emma, a couple of days later.

"Shhh," Phyllis warned when they shrieked in surprise and delight, but it was too late. They didn't hear Levina approaching until she was standing in her daughter's upstairs bedroom doorway.

"Where on earth did you get that?" Levina said the word "that" like she had seen something disgusting. "It's smut," Levina said. "It's not something nice girls should look at."

Phyllis confessed. Phyllis pleaded.

"Please let me keep it; please."

Levina absconded with the magazine, but later bargained with her daughter.

"Keep it if you must," Levina said, in a disgusted tone, "but you will have to draw clothes on every single naked body." Phyllis promised to cloth the nudists, but she didn't say when.

Levina evidently forgot about it because it was not mentioned again. Phyllis wondered if Levina told Aunt Marie and if so, what Marie said to her boys. Kenny and Jerry found lots of good stuff at the Chittenango dump. Phyllis assumed that was the source of the nudist magazines. *(When Kenny was 80 he confessed to the existence of the magazines that had, indeed, come from the dump).*

Back then, Chittenango dump was not a smelly, rotting place like people think of village dumps. Folks fed food scraps to animals and composted vegetable matter. People disposed of old magazines and furniture at the dump and sometimes tossed valuable antiques and other treasures without realizing it. Kenny and Jerry were clever dump pickers and found possessions that Aunt Marie displayed in her home, saying "one man's trash is another man's treasure."

"I haven't seen you write in your new diary," Levina said before supper one July afternoon. "Don't you like it?"

It wasn't that Phyllis didn't like the diary, she had stuck it in her desk drawer and forgot about it. She retrieved the journal and made the first entry on July 23:

"I made my first cake today, we had it for supper. It was good. Mother took me to see the movie The Yearling. I loved it. It was sad. On the way home we saw the famous Flying Saucers in the sky, but no one knows what they are."

(The first reports of UFO's, unidentified flying objects, appeared in newspapers in June 1947 after a pilot in Boise, Idaho reported seeing disc-shaped lights in the sky. There are many theories, but no substantial proof to explain the phenomena).

Levina checked her daughter's diary entries, making corrections as though it was home work. She read her stories with the eye of a censor, editing out every swear word and suggesting she substitute darn and heck for damn and hell. She never took the Lord's name in vain; she had learned that much in Sunday School. But having listened to her father and his friends, the little girl was well schooled in the art of cussing; and real men did not use darn and heck. Nevertheless she could not convince her mother that accuracy was important. Levina didn't seem to "get" that diaries were private. Nor did it occur to her that her daughter might have secrets. Not until she hid her diary. Phyllis knew her mother had looked because she got a note asking why she was "shutting her mother out of her life." Phyllis left her diary hidden, and

162

ignored her mother's note just as any writer would have done.

The Cazenovia School building was bursting at the seams that fall and both sixth grade sections of around 35 pupils each attended classes in a large room on the second floor of the brick Municipal Building that was located downtown. Miss Lee taught one section and Miss Putnam the other. They worked through the problems of having two classes in one large room by arranging book cases between the sections.

The fire department was housed on the ground floor.

Sixth grade bus students disembarked from their separate buses and boarded the sixth grade bus for the ride down town. "Roll Me Over in the Clover," they sang lustily every day.

"Pipe down!" yelled the driver. There were snickers and stifled laugher, but not for long. The next day it was the same, "Roll me over, lay me down and do it again."

"I said pipe down!" the driver demanded again and again like it was a game.

Phyllis loved their pudgy, red-faced teacher, Miss Putnam, who favored country kids and was not averse to putting the so-called "rich kids" in their place. Sixth grade was the best year ever.

Phyllis wrote stories for fun. Friends read her stories, and teachers encouraged her to continue writing. The highlight of the year for Phyllis was the play she wrote and produced. It was called "Horses," and that's all she remembers. Students donned burlap bags with two corners tied to represent ears. There was a large stage in the center of the room and Miss Putnam's class performed the play for Miss Lee's class while Phyllis basked in the role of playwright and producer.

Erwin sat hunched over in his rocking chair listening intently to the final minutes of the 1947 World Series on the radio when Phyllis got home from school. Erwin rooted for the Yankees with fervor, to the detriment of his fingernails that were chewed down to the quick. The Dodgers had won game six, forcing the seventh and deciding game at Yankee Stadium in Bronx, New York on that October 6.

"They did it. The Yanks did it. Damned if they didn't," Erwin proclaimed with pride as he headed to the barn for afternoon chores. Levina bustled around the kitchen, oblivious to the baseball game. Phyllis changed her clothes and joined her father in the barn where he was singing a duet of "Now is the Hour" with Bing Crosby that blared from the barn radio. She loved hearing her father sing, but not her mother.

Levina only sang in church. She embarrassed Phyllis by singing loud and *trilling* the notes. Phyllis thought it was because she was Dutch. Levina sang "Silent Night" in Dutch at the church Christmas program every single year. She never tired of telling the story about her family emigrating from Holland in 1912.

Erwin was still glowing from the Yankee's victory when he came to the house for supper.

"I guess we showed them Dodgers. They thought they were a shoo-in with that new hot-shot nigger player of theirs. Too bad, huh?"

"Erwin!" Levina said using her self-righteous voice. "The word is Negro."

"Good meatloaf, Ma." Erwin had a way of seeming very serious when he was teasing. He was good at it.

The African American player was Jackie Robinson who made integration history earlier that year when he joined the Brooklyn Dodgers as the first Major League Negro player.

Autumn colors mingled like an impressionist painting on the easel of rolling hills surrounding Perryville. It was a magnificent October when you inhale deeply to capture the fragrance of the season. Indian summer was short and meant to be savored. The hardest part of the work year was almost over and people were in high spirits.

The monster threshing machine arrived at the farm the middle of the month. The machine was too expensive to be owned by one farmer, so threshing was a cooperative effort. Three or four neighboring farmers worked together spending a day at each farm harvesting the grain and sharing the expense of the machine and the operator.

When the kernels were full and the straw was golden colored, Erwin cut the oats with his harvester machine that ejected bundles of grain called sheaves, tied together with twine. The bundles were picked up with pitch forks and set up in the field leaning together like little wigwams to dry. When the threshing machine arrived, the sheaves were stacked on hay wagons and pulled by a team of horses to where the threshing machine was set up near the barn.

The big, sheet-metal machine the size of a tractor trailer that resembled something out of the Wizard of Oz, groaned, shook and belched clouds of dust as the sheaves disappeared into the innards of the beast. Somehow it separated the grain from the chaff amid much rattling and shaking. The straw was blown out into a pile and the grain poured out of another spout. Men took turns holding burlap bags under the spout to catch the grain, and tying the bags closed. The bulging bags were carried over strong shoulders to wooden grain bins in the barn where they were poured out and stored in bulk.

The oats in the bin felt cool and smooth to the touch. Phyllis and neighbor kids who came along with their parents laughed as they tried to walk upright in piles of oats that shifted like grains of sand. Falling down was the most fun because it didn't hurt at all. Little pieces of leaves sometimes stuck to the grain. If it was poison ivy, the kids broke out in a rash. It was all in a day's play. As needed to feed the cows throughout the year, the oats were once again bagged up and trucked to the grist mill to be ground into mash. A truck owned by the mill picked up the grain and delivered the grist.

Chatty wives wearing cotton house dresses and aprons in bright prints trimmed with colorful rickrack worked together cooking huge meals for the ravenous threshers who ate at large dining room tables. Full bib aprons were standard uniform for farm women who wore a clean, starched apron every day. They peeled piles of potatoes, roasted pork, warmed sauerkraut, thickened rich brown gravy, cracked open huge Hubbard squash with an axe and cooked the orange vegetable sprinkled with brown sugar. They shared gossip, laughed, opened jars of homemade apple sauce, made biscuits and pies, exchanged recipes, wiped sweaty brows, rounded up children who were running around excitedly trying, or not trying, to stay out of trouble.

Levina ground her own strong horseradish roots from plants that grew along the foundation of the house. Phyllis helped her mother pick apples from trees that grew out by the silo to make applesauce, eagerly biting into bruised sections of apples that tasted like cider. Phyllis learned how to cook, not by instruction, but by example. She could whip up a full meal at an early age without even thinking about what she was doing. Levina called it second nature.

The women fed the kids in the kitchen and when the men and children were done eating the exhausted but happy wives ate dinner, then cleaned up the kitchen and planned the next day's menu. If the weather cooperated and it did not rain, the threshing was over in several days.

Autumn prayers pleaded for a bumper crop and a dry harvest.

Snow arrived on November 8.

"It's too blasted cold for this time of year," Erwin complained when he came in from the barn for breakfast. "Damn, I miss good old Southern California."

He hung his barn frock on a wall hook behind the stove and rubbed his cold, sore hands over the hot kitchen range.   After washing his hands with Lava soap, he reached for the bottle of rose water and glycerin that the Chittenango pharmacist mixed especially for him. The aroma of the lotion tickled Phyllis's nose as her father massaged it into his rough hands and cracked fingers.

"Three guinea hens froze last night. Foolish things are too stupid to roost in the barn," Erwin said.

Guinea hens roosted in the old maple tree that grew at the corner of the farmhouse outside Phyllis's bedroom window. She heard them most nights calling "buck wheat, buck wheat," or so it seemed.

"Ashes to ashes, dust to dust," Erwin said tossing their carcasses onto the cold fields along with fresh manure.

Eleven - 1948

**Erwin, Donna, Phyllis, Dan
and Donald**

A monstrous sheet metal forced air coal furnace replaced two pot belly stoves in 1948. Central heating did not extend to the second floor, but Phyllis didn't mind sleeping in her igloo-like bedroom. Every morning she heard her father shake the furnace grates and add more coal. Her life was punctuated by comforting sounds and smells.

Dashing up the frigid stairway to her frigid room at night, "Phyll" (her current name preference) kicked off her slippers and slid under the blankets between soft flannel sheets. She got a whiff of scorched newspaper and stretched her toes to the warm spot at the foot of her bed. "Ahhh," she sighed, resting her feet close to the hot soapstone. The only visible part of Phyllis was her nose. Her bedroom took on a mystical aura with window panes etched in a sparkling jungle of frost ferns seemingly created by the feathery wings of angels.

Phyll's soapstone that was as smooth as marble, spent every winter day absorbing oven heat from the kitchen coal stove. At bedtime her mom gingerly wrapped the blistering hot 12 by 10-inch rectangular stone in several layers of newspaper and torn flannel sheets, and dashed upstairs to her daughter's room where she slipped the bed warmer between the sheets at the foot of the bed. By morning the soapstone, wrapped like a mummy in layers of scorched brown fabric and newspaper, had cooled down, but the middle of the bed was still cozy. The trick was to lie still.

"David wrote me a love letter today," Phyllis confided to her diary on January 21, 1948. "It was wonderful. To tell the truth, I wrote him one, too." It was the first of many letters David wrote in neat script on blue decorative note cards that he borrowed from his mother's desk. He mailed the letters at Perryville Post Office for three cents each.

Phyllis saw David for the first time when she walked self-consciously into Perryville School on opening day of third grade. She was the new kid in school that

September--shy, frightened, awkward and friendless. Four rows of desks for grades one through four were lined up one behind the other. Kindergarten was not offered. Children started school at age six. David sat in the second row because he was in second grade. Phyllis was in third grade. He was the best-dressed kid in school. Levina said he was "as neat as a pin." His clothes were clean and pressed, his hair was freshly trimmed and he had a smile like an angel. The other kids stared at Phyllis making faces, whispering, snickering or ignoring her entirely. David smiled.

David and Phyllis became best friends. They rode their bikes around the village, took hikes, and bought ice cream in Dixie Cups at the general store. Exploring the wilderness near the top of thundering Perryville Falls they scraped at foundations of old buildings with archeological fervor.

"Maybe this was the milk factory," David said, walking along a field stone foundation, "because it's close to the railroad." Gone was the black smith shop, rail road station, saloon, and hotel; who knows what all. One of the foundations was tall with openings for doors and windows. They imagined a little old man sitting inside sending telegrams.

They decided the grist mill had been built next to the mill pond where a water wheel would have powered the grinding stones

They walked the Lehigh Valley railroad tracks balancing on the rails like tight rope walkers. When the daily freight train consisting of four cars came down the tracks, they waved at the engineer in the locomotive and the conductor who stood at the end of the caboose. They sat together at community suppers and held hands in the dark watching movies that the Methodist minister projected on a big white screen. They ice skated on the frozen pond up the hill behind Erwin's cow barn and slid down the long hill on runner sleds lying on their tummies with snow blasting their reddened faces. And best of all they were Valentines.

They stopped at old Jay's farm just down the road from the Lambert's if they saw him outside, because he loved telling tales, and they loved listening to them. He knew a lot about the old days, and was always eager to tell another story. He'd spit tobacco juice, wipe his mustache with his shirt sleeve, and begin.

"In the ole days, that lil' house next ta the church was half the saloon," he said, the other half is the third house from church. Beats me how they done it, but's the hones' ta god truth," he said taking a spit of tobacco juice. Jay said he dasn't drink, mind ya, but he knew plenty did an' t'weren't all. "Yes-siree," he vowed, "plenty ah mischief of ah Saturday night in them good ole days."

"Do youse all know how Chit-ten-an-go got that name?" Jay waited for the children to answer with a mischievous twinkle in his eyes.

They shook their heads indicating they didn't know.

"Well, I'll tell youse," he said, spitting tobacco juice out of the corner of his mouth. "Way the hell back ah ole trapper rascal was wand-ring down by the creek. T'weren't no village or nuttin' back then. His flea-bitten ole hound kept stoppin' an' smellin' an' the ole fella got sick'n'tired of waiting. So he goes an' says real disgusted like: 'For god's sake will ya just 'shit 'n then go.' Damned if the moniker didn't sure 'nuf stick." Jay laughed but Phyllis and David just looked at each other. Phyllis would not tell her mother that story.

Donna grew chubbier and more fun by the day. Even before her first birthday on February 3, she climbed up the stairs, but sat at the top afraid to venture back down.

When Phyllis got home from school on Donna's birthday she bundled the little girl up like an Eskimo

171

and took her outside. The toddler squealed in delight as big sister ran along the road between mini mountain ranges of snow from their house to Jay's and back pulling the runner sled. Overhead, electric wires hummed in the frigid weather like a colossal bee hive. Bowser followed along, sniffing at every yellow stain in the snow, tracking neighborhood dogs, and adding some additional color of his own. After supper the family sang "Happy Birthday," and Donna stuck her fingers in the pink icing and stuffed them into her pudgy, little mouth.

Winter slid slowly into spring, sluggish as a toboggan in deep, soft snow. The snowdrops were the first sign. The vernal equinox had come and gone, but it was still winter where the Lamberts lived. A fierce March wind peppered with ice crystals nudged Phyll's skinny body into the warmth of the country kitchen as she pushed open the weathered back door from the wood shed. Coffee steamed and oatmeal bubbled on her mother's white enamel cook stove.

Phyllis, where is your father?" Levina had meticulous timing but not a lot of patience. When breakfast was ready she expected her family to be seated at the table.

"He's coming," said Phyllis, who sometimes helped her father with morning barn chores when she didn't have to catch the school bus. "There's a new calf."

Stanchions fit loosely around cows' necks and opened and closed like huge safety pins. The animals could stand, lie down and move a little from side to side, but backward and forward motion was limited. Erwin's small barn did not have a birthing area, so when a cow calved in the barn it happened in the stanchion, sometimes with the mother still standing. Calves made messy appearances after much grunting and hard breathing on the part of the mother.

172

Phyllis was flabbergasted the first time she saw a cow give birth, not that it happened, but that something as big as a calf could fit inside the cow's body. Sometimes Erwin had to reach inside the mother cow with his bare arm to straighten a calf. Phyllis thought it was funny seeing her father straddling the gutter, leaning against the cow's rear end with his right arm inside the cow. Sometimes he tied a rope to a calf's legs to pull it out, but usually the slimy, bloody calves slid out with the cow's last grunt and push of labor.

Erwin cut and tied the umbilical cord, washed the calf that was struggling to stand up with warm water and moved it to the calf pen where the older calves eyed it with curiosity.

Smelling the blood, stealthy barn cats appeared from all directions eyeing the afterbirth in the gutter. Tearing at the mass of tissue, they ran away with pieces of the delicacy.

Erwin recorded breeding dates, as best he could estimate, by ear tag number in a small "Farmers' POCKET LEDGER," compliments of N.G. Deppoliti & Sons, Canastota, N.Y. The small almanac held useful information for farmers, a detailed list of John Deere farm equipment and blank pages for stock-breeding records. He kept the stained, fly specked notebook on a barn window sill next to the teat ointment. He had a good idea when each calf was expected and kept a close eye especially on first-calf heifers.

If labor seemed difficult or took too long, Erwin summoned a veterinarian. The vet sometimes shoved both arms up the cow's birth canal. An occasional dead calf, poor thing, lay lifeless on the barn floor. Black Sam, the Jewish cattle dealer, took the bodies and Phyllis wondered what he did with them. Levina said maybe they were processed into dog food.

Fresh cows were not allowed to nuzzle or nurse their babies. They strained in their stanchions, rolling their eyes, bellowing and contorting their bodies trying to see their calves. Sometimes twin calves were born which was twice as amazing to Phyllis. Milk cows were bred back every year in order to continue milk production. Healthy heifer calves were kept and raised; bull calves were sold.

Summer calves born in the pasture had the luxury of spending a few hours with their moms before Erwin went looking for a cow that did not appear at the barn with the herd. Erwin picked up the calf and loaded it on a wagon taking it to the barn. Phyllis usually went along. The desperate mother ran along the pasture fence as fast as she could, her distended bag swinging from side to side with milk dripping from her teats. The distressed animal bellowed in such a mournful way that Phyllis wanted to cry.

The mother cow's rich milk, called colostrum, was fed to the new calves for the first few days. Colostrum contains antibodies to protect the newborn against disease, as well as being low in fat and high in protein. Calves were taught to drink by forcing their muzzles into a pail of warm milk while holding one hand under the milk with fingers pointed upwards. The calves naturally sucked the fingers with much slurping and drizzling and swallowed milk at the same time. Soon they were drinking from a pail on their own.

"It's a bull calf, darn it," Phyllis said. "I'll get him to suck after breakfast." Phyllis was sad because she knew Black Sam would buy the bull calf for somebody's veal cutlets.

"Oh dear," Levina lamented, sticking a spoon into the oatmeal. "It's too thick." She spooned congealed cereal into her daughter's bowl. Phyllis added creamy milk, brown sugar and raisins. She turned up her nose at the small bowl of slimy, homemade canned rhubarb sauce

174

that was supposedly so good for her. Maybe so, but it was terribly sour even though her mother added sugar. Donna sat in the second-hand high chair that Aunt Marie had delivered, stuffing small pieces of toast into her mouth. "Be happy you don't have to eat rhubarb," Phyllis whispered.

"Was there any sign of snowdrops under the lilac bush?" Levina was anxious for the appearance of delicate, white bell-shaped flowers that bloomed in the snow. Everyone in the family was expected to keep the vigil. Phyllis had forgotten to look that morning.

"I wish your father would hurry. The coffee will be like mud." She gave the oatmeal another stir, removed her glasses and wiped her face with the hem of her apron. It was hot work cooking over a coal stove, and Levina was prone to hot flashes. Her face had a moist, rosy glow as she forced air upward from her mouth like a bellows for relief from the heat. She poured a cup of coffee, plopped herself into a chair, drummed the table with the fingers of one rough hand in exasperation and pushed damp graying hair off her forehead with the other. Levina would not admit she was tired of winter, because she always claimed to love the season, but she was showing signs of winter weariness.

"The problem with life," Levina sighed, "it is so daily." Phyllis did not yet understand what her mother meant, but the time would come when she would.

The door opened and Erwin walked into the kitchen accompanied by a blast of frigid air. Snow stuck to the brim of his denim cap, but he had a smile on his face.

"Look what I've got, Ma." He held a small bunch of delicate white flowers in his leather gloves.

"Snowdrops." She whispered the words like a prayer. Spring could not be far behind.

Spring arrived in its own time, and with the season came more new calves. Phyllis heard Black Sam's noisy truck rumble into the driveway in a cloud of dust early on a Saturday morning in late May. She closed her mind to the abduction of yet another bull calf. Erwin said at breakfast that Sam was excited about the establishment of the Jewish State of Israel. Erwin, who loved a good political debate, had stirred the pot.

"What about the war?" Erwin asked the Jewish cattle dealer. Egypt, Iraq, Jordan, Lebanon and Syria had attacked Israel. Black Sam said Palestine was "The Promised Land."

"Tell that to the Arabs," Erwin said.

(War commenced upon the termination of the British Mandate of Palestine on May 15. The Jews called it the War of Independence, but thousands of Arab citizens that were displaced from their homes called it a catastrophe).

"Did you notice the lilacs this morning?" Levina asked. "The whole yard is fragrant."

Lilac blossoms seemingly opened overnight, bursting into white, lavender and deep purple blooms. On Decoration Day, Levina filled quart jars with spring flowers and left them on her parents' graves. Red and yellow tulips with crown-shaped blossoms preceded the lilacs by a few days. Soon bright yellow daffodils and jonquils would join the spring parade nodding their pretty heads in the garden.

It was an ordinary day, but it turned out to be one of the most exciting of Phyllis's life. Erwin had his nose stuck in the newspaper while Levina and Phyllis cleared away lunch dishes when they heard the loud rumble of an airplane buzzing the house. Running outside Phyllis saw the small plane swooping low overhead tipping its wings. Somehow Erwin knew it was his nephew, Donald Lambert, waving from the cockpit. It was the first time one of their relatives had arrived by plane.

"Let's go for an aero-plane ride," Erwin said with a huge grin.

The family piled into the car and Erwin drove to the farm on Perryville-Chittenango Road, where his brother, Herbert's family lived before moving to Pennsylvania. Cousin Donald was Herbert's son. The property belonged to Dr. Luther, a Syracuse dentist who owned a private plane and had a landing strip next to his house. Cousin Donald and his friend, Dan, who owned the visiting airplane, stood waiting when they arrived.

"Wanna go for a ride?" Cousin Donald asked.

Phyllis was first in line.

Donald took off into the spring sky with Phyllis in the second seat. Her heart raced as the plane soared and flew low over the countryside sprinkled with farms. Phyllis was thrilled with her bird's eye view, and was pretty sure she was the first of her friends to ride in a plane. She couldn't wait to tell them. Cousin Donald tossed a package out the window that floated down to someone who seemed to be waiting. It was mysterious like a story book. He flew over Perryville and their farm and let Phyllis steer the plane for a few minutes before landing again and taking Erwin for a spin. Levina said no thanks.

"It was the most fun I've ever had," she told her mother. "I'm going to learn how to fly." She would brag to her friends about steering a real airplane boasting that she wasn't scared at all.

"No more pencils, no more books, no more teachers' dirty looks, and when the teacher rings the bell, drop your books and run like heck," the bus kids sang on the last day of school in late June. They said heck instead of hell even if it didn't rhyme. Phyllis was sad that sixth grade was over. It was her absolutely favorite school year. Getting off the school bus, she ran into the house anxious to read the comic strips. She grabbed a couple of Lorna Doone shortbread cookies and plunked down in the kitchen rocking chair to read *Brenda Starr, Star Reporter*. Brenda's mysterious, tall, handsome suitor, Basil St. John, who wore a black patch over one eye, sent Brenda rare black orchids. It was exciting, but Phyllis could not pay attention to the story that day because her itching head was driving her crazy. It had started after lunch. Levina said maybe she was allergic to the new shampoo until Phyllis scratched furiously, trapping a tiny bug under her fingernail.

"Mom, what's this?"

"My word," Levina exclaimed examining the creature, "you've got lice! Where have you been? Did you go to that barn again?" Some of Phyll's friends gathered in an old carriage house in Perryville for secret club meetings. Phyllis was guilty as charged although Levina had asked her not to go there.

"What must I do to prevent you from going there again!" Levina said in a pleading tone intended to shame her daughter. Phyllis doubted that was where she got bugs, but Levina was adamant. Within the Perryville caste system, there were certain families that Levina frowned upon. She didn't want her daughter playing with "those" children and she wouldn't eat food "those families" brought to church suppers.

Levina carried a wooden kitchen chair to the back lawn and placed it under the big maple tree. It was the only tree in the back yard, and many activities took place under its leafy canopy. The smaller maples in the front yard did not have the same status.

Phyllis pouted and muttered as Levina cut through her long braids with a pair of shears. Using a tried-and-true

178

method, she poured foul-smelling, oily kerosene through what remained of her daughter's thick, dark hair. Phyllis was absolutely positive every person in every car and truck that drove past the house knew she had cooties. After the coal oil treatment, Levina drove her daughter to her friend Jean's house in Chittenango for a Toni home permanent. Jean was a beautician who worked out of her own home. Levina was hoping the strong chemicals in the home permanent solution would kill the little buggers.

"There are still nits in the hairline," Jean whispered to Levina.

Why were they whispering? It wasn't as though she didn't know she had lice. Adults lowered their voices when talking about taboo subjects even if no one else was there. Having bugs was very embarrassing. Supposedly only dirty people got lice.

The worst part of the whole experience was ending up with a head full of tight curls that she absolutely hated. She had to pretend she liked them because she didn't want to admit to her friends the real reason she got a haircut and a permanent.

Phyllis lugged the manual reel lawn mower out of the tool shed and pushed it toward the lawn. A metal cylinder mounted between the wheels held the blades with a thick wooden handle sticking up from the framework. Pushing with all her might on the handle the cylinder rotated moving the heavy blades that cut the grass. It was fairly easy pushing the heavy mower on the driveway, but getting it through a lawn that was mostly weeds, was tough. Erwin said it was good for her, and that it developed muscles. Phyllis called it "kid power."

She pushed the contraption through grass on the back lawn cutting "D.T.," David's initials in the grass before mowing the rest of the lawn. It took all her strength to keep the circular blades rotating. Taking a break after finishing the large initials, she nibbled on the sweet tender inside stem of a tall blade of grass. It tasted like asparagus.

Bowser barked at a car pulling into the driveway and wagged his tail when he saw Julia and Art. Art was on vacation from the factory where he worked, and a day driving the tractor in Erwin's hayfield was fun for him. Levina came out of the house carrying Donna to greet the visitors.

The sweet scent of dry hay hung like cologne on the summer air as Art raked the hay in the field next to the house, leaving a cloud of dust behind him. Raking fluffed the hay into windrows so the hay loader could pick it up. Bowser ran along the side of the tractor, sniffing out mice that ran helter-skelter from under the hay.

Levina and Julia sat on kitchen chairs under the big maple tree shelling peas for supper. Earlier that day, Levina had yelled to Phyllis to run to the edge of the road to grab a bunch of pea vines off a truck that was driving up the road heading for the canning factory in Canastota. She was lucky that day running close to the truck and grabbing enough pea vines to make a good mess of peas for supper. She thought the truck driver slowed down when he saw her because he smiled and waved. Levina was very fond of fresh peas, even if they were stolen. She served them swimming in warm, buttery milk seasoned with salt and pepper.

Phyllis listened to the women gossip while she kept an eye on her little sister. Levina had promised Art a salt pork supper. *"Oh Goody,"* Phyllis thought facetiously. She could not stomach fried pork fat which was all it was. Levina coated chunks of salt pork in seasoned flour and fried them crisp and brown on the outside. She served it with mashed potatoes, white gravy, and her home ground horseradish that was so strong it brought tears to people's eyes. *"Yuck, yuck,"* was all Phyllis could think. Levina would want her to eat a small piece, but she would push it under the potatoes and then give it to Bowser.

"Jean and Don are having a party," Julia said "and you're invited." Julia's sister Jean had married well. So well, in fact, that they owned St. Helena Island. It was one of the so-called Thousand Islands located in the St. Lawrence River that separated the United States and Canada.

"Just wait until you see their 'little cottage," Julia said. Julia's brother-in-law, Don, owned a hardware store in Syracuse and a large home on James Street where the well-to-do lived. Phyllis knew they were rich. People had to be rich to own an island. She didn't know why Julia's well-to-do relatives included the not-so-well-to-do Lamberts on their party guest lists. They had attended a previous party at their home in Syracuse. Don, an amateur magician, performed tricks for the guests. The invitation to St. Helena Island arrived the following week.

Erwin rarely took a day off, but being invited to St. Helena was a special occasion. His friend, Clate, and a neighbor boy would cover Saturday night and Sunday morning chores. Suitcases were packed and waiting when Erwin came in for breakfast.

"You guys in hurry?" he asked.

"Fill her up," Erwin said to the man at the gas station who had an ESSO insignia embroidered on the shirt pocket of his neat uniform. While the car was filling with gasoline, the man checked the oil, washed the windshield and kicked tires to see if they needed air. It took 13 gallons to fill the gas tank and cost $1.82. Erwin handed Levina change from $2.00 and a sheet of S&H green stamps. Phyllis was the one who pasted the stamps in redemption books and leafed through the catalog. When they had enough stamps for something they wanted, they went shopping for free at the Sperry and Hutchinson Redemption Center.

Erwin didn't drive fast and with nearly one hundred miles ahead of them Phyllis made up a story imagining life on the river. She thought about Tom Sawyer and Huckleberry Finn on the Mississippi wondering if it would be possible to have a raft on the St. Lawrence.

Goody, Phyllis thought seeing a succession of ubiquitous Burma Shave signs along the road. She read each sign aloud as the car rolled past.

>*A man,*
>*A miss,*
>*A car,*
>*A curve.*
>*He kissed the miss,*
>*And missed the curve.*
>*Burma Shave.*

St. Helena Island located on the river narrows at Brown Bay and Swan Bay, was within shouting distance of the mainland. Erwin parked the car, and they walked to the dock carrying their suitcases.

Someone on the island waved, and jumped into the motor launch. The boat engine made deep, guttural sounds; chug, chug, chug as it pulled up to the dock. Phyllis could see her reflection in the polished wood.

"Hi," said Don, who owned the boat and the island. "Welcome to St. Helena."

Phyllis couldn't wait to get to the island. Julia was right. The house was too big to be called a cottage. Phyllis decided it was a magic mansion. Painted white with green trim and a red roof, the house was perched smack dab in the center of the small island. There were extra angles to the tall roof and porches jutted out in several directions. The boat house next to the river matched the house. An American flag waved from the top of a tall flagpole that was surrounded by pine trees and hard woods. It was a most enchanting place, and just for the weekend, it was Phyllis's very own special island.

Phyllis doesn't remember what was served for dinner at the anniversary party or how many people were there. What she remembers is the proud expression on Levina's face when Jean and Don raved about her clever gift of freshly dressed chickens. Levina had not known what else they could give people who had just about everything. On the card Levina wrote that she would deliver dressed chickens whenever they wanted them. Don said they would enjoy a drive to the farm.

The fantasy life of Phyllis Lambert shifted into high gear that night when she was shown to her very own room. The wide St. Lawrence River shimmered in moonlight. Phyllis imagined herself as Brenda Starr, Star Reporter, on an assignment. She fell asleep lost in a romantic dream-world and woke up Sunday morning to see a really big ship steaming right past her bedroom window. "Wow! Wow!" She could not wait to tell her friends about it.

Casowasco, a sprawling, wooded estate on Owasco Lake in Central New York, was the former summer home of Theodore Case who invented Movietone Sound-on film. The estate was given to the Methodist Church after his death in 1944. When the estate became a church camp, the three large rustic brown-shingled buildings were named after towns in Israel. The largest mansion named Galilee, was closest to the lake. The others were Nazareth and Emmaus. Phyllis liked Galilee the best, and was happy that she was assigned to stay there.

Phyllis attended camp at Casowasco for the first time that summer and continued for the next three years. A letter from Levina was waiting when Phyllis arrived. Her mother wrote every single day. Phyllis did not get homesick, but the letters implied that she might. Typical of young campers at that time, she mailed letters and postcards home even though she was only away for a week.

Bunk beds were packed into various sized bedrooms. Rowdy pillow fights, ghost stories and true confessions were nightly rituals. Self-confident popular girls with nicknames like Mickey and Mikey, whispered stories with sexual innuendo and bragged about their experiences with boys. Phyllis talked about her cute boyfriend David, but the girls didn't seem to believe her.

She had a crush on a young German staff member named Wolfgang. He even let her take his picture. Heart throb Wolfgang taught the campers a folk song that they belted out in various accents and mispronunciations. Seven decades later, Phyllis still hears the song in her head.

Du, du liegst mir im Herzen, Du, du liegst mir im Sinn, Du, du machst mir viel Schmerzen, weißt nicht wie gut ich dir bin. Ja, ja, ja, ja, weifst nicht wie gut ich dir bin.

Days were filled with bible study, group discussions, craft projects, hikes, dining hall duty, games, swimming, and free time. Sitting around roaring camp fires after dark watching logs crackle and explode in sparks, campers were challenged to be better Christians as they sang the Negro spiritual, "Kum ba yah."

"Kum ba yah, Lord, Kum ba yah," (come by here). They sang enthusiastically feeling the Spirit of the Lord in the mist that rose from the lake. "Are Ye Able" was by far the favorite camp hymn. "Are ye able, said the Master, to be crucified with Me? Yea, the sturdy dreamers answered, to the death we follow Thee. Lord, we are able, our spirits are Thine. Remold them, make us, like Thee, divine. Thy guiding radiance above us shall be a beacon to God, to love and loyalty."

Young voices blended in youthful Christian fervor, caught up in the moment, and in the beauty and tranquility of their surroundings. They sang "Are Ye Able" nightly, sincerely believing every word. When Taps echoed through the quiet camp, each one prayed silently. They would be transformed people when they returned to their home churches. They would be leaders for Christ. They just knew it.

The Smiths, who were Grange friends from Chittenango showed up at supper time, as usual, to buy eggs. Of course, Levina invited them to eat. That was just the way it was. The Lamberts often had company, but Erwin and Levina rarely visited folks because they were always too busy.

Phyllis and the Smith kids, Nancy and Bobby, played hide and go seek while supper was being cooked. Phyllis, who had the advantage, squeezed into Silver's stall where the other kids wouldn't dare venture. She climbed into the manger and gazed at cob web-draped rafters above the stalls daydreaming as she often did. Silver munched hay around her, not minding the company. That was when she noticed something wedged between hand-hewn beams; something large and brown, and covered in dust. It took a few minutes before she realized what it was.

"It's a saddle!" she yelled revealing her hiding place in one shout, "I found a saddle."

It was a mystery, that saddle. And even more surprising, the belly strap fit around Silver's wide girth.

Silver loved to gallop and Phyllis loved to ride. It was a perfect match. The big horse with a tawny coat and silver mane and tail galloped across the pasture so fast it frightened Levina who stood by the fence cautioning her daughter. "Slow down, be careful. Be careful; you'll fall." Phyllis had no intention of slowing down the enormous galloping horse as she flew across the pasture like Pegasus. At last she had her very own riding horse.

"Fall is in the air," Levina said as she hung clothes on a web of line crisscrossing the back lawn. Gold, rust and burgundy colored chrysanthemums exploded into bloom. Betty coasted her bicycle all the way to Perryville on her way to Phyll's house for one more visit before school. She would need to push her bike back up the two-mile hill to get home. They had plans for the day that did not include babysitting.

The girls glanced over their shoulders as they ventured into Erwin's corn field and disappeared into a world devoid of parental restraint. Long rows of verdant six-foot tall stalks formed a camouflaged hideout for errant 12-year-olds with clandestine homemade cigarettes. They rolled their own cigs just like movie cowboys. Standing far inside the corn maze with only the blue sky visible, they broke out of their humdrum rural existence.

Phyllis took a crumbled paper lunch bag out of her pocket and pulled out two very poor excuses for cigarettes.

"More Doctors smoke CAMELS than any other cigarette," she mimicked a tobacco company advertisement.

The girls stood between the rows and lighted their fags made from crushed, dried maple leaves rolled tightly in strips of newspaper. The home-made cigarettes burned too fast and tasted terrible. They coughed on the smoke, laughed and watched big, green grasshoppers jump from stalk to stalk. They would have to come up with another plan if they wanted to smoke, because maple leaves were not the answer.

BRANGGGG!!   The bell for passing of classes reverberated through the school hallways in a series of discordant blasts.   Phyllis left the safety of her seventh grade home room, joining the crush of students in the hallway.

"Well, hello there," Eddie said in a flirty way. He leaned against the hall lockers as though he had all the time in the world, and ran a comb through his thick, dark hair flipping it into a peacock crest. Phyllis forced a quick half smile and forged on through the crowd. The last thing she wanted to do was draw attention to her shy self by being late for class.

"Welcome to Junior High" was scrawled in yellow chalk on the black board of her first class. Phyll opened her new zippered, three-ring notebook. There were tabs for each subject and pockets on the inside of the front and back covers. A note from her mother was tucked in one of the pockets. It was one of the ubiquitous notes that Phyllis got from Levina with words of wisdom. Honestly, she was tired of them. Didn't her mother realize she needed growing room?

Twelve – 1949

**Home Sweet Home,
Perryville, New York**

Phyllis and Betty sat at the semi-circle vinyl-covered booth in Betty's mother's spacious kitchen on the first Saturday of the year. They polished their nails while waiting for the meeting to begin. Betty's mother, Edna, and a neighbor, Iva, had organized the Adventures 4-H Club. The 4-H was a youth organization of the Cooperative State Research, Education and Extension Service of the United States Department of Agriculture. Edna laughed at the long title on the correspondence she received sanctioning the club.

"I lose my breath just reading that long title." Edna laughed easily and watching her made the girls laugh too.

Every sleep-over at Betty's house was an adventure. Betty's father, Walt, operated a mega-sized dairy farm where everything was on a scale at least four times larger and noisier than Erwin's. The large-family home life was raucous in comparison to her own quiet existence. The birth of six children in nine-years guaranteed a lively household.

Walt often rested in the downstairs bedroom, stretched out on the double bed with the door open to the dining room. Edna curled up next to him in a seductive way, playfully massaging her husband. Phyllis could not stop gawking the first time she noticed their behavior. She had never seen her parents kiss or embrace much less cuddle. Edna, an attractive red head, was fourteen years younger than Levina. Edna was impulsive and fun; the antithesis of Levina who was sanctimonious, solemn and no-nonsense.

Iva breezed in with a few more girls and the meeting was called to order. The girls sat in the living room trying to concentrate while Iva explained the mission of the 4-H Club between deep drags on a cigarette and a hacky cough.

"Engaging youth to reach their fullest potential while advancing the field of youth development," she read from a booklet.

"Huh?" Phyllis whispered to Betty. "What the heck?" The girls exchanged mirthful glances stifling giggles.

"The four H's stand for head, heart, hands and health," Iva said. The first order of business was memorizing the 4-H Pledge that was written on a large, green four-leaf clover poster. They girls read the motto in unison.

I pledge my Head to clearer thinking, my Heart to greater loyalty, my Hands to larger service and my Health to better living, for my club my community and my country.

The club projects for that year were: "Let's Have a Party," "Learning to Sew," and "Food Preservation." Each girl was expected to give a demonstration. Iva came up with the idea of Phyllis making a winter salad using artistically arranged canned vegetables. Fresh vegetables were scarce during the winter.

Phyllis wrote the demonstration with Iva's help and practiced arranging canned green beans, yellow beans, carrots, beets, peas and baby potatoes artistically on a platter. Her spiel included information about dietary requirements and the health benefits of vegetables. Demonstration day was scheduled for April 9 and she wanted it to be perfect.

"You've got a letter from David," Levina said as Phyllis walked through the door after getting off the school bus on a brisk February afternoon. Levina's smile displayed the gold tooth she usually tried to hide. Phyllis took the letter upstairs to read and tucked it in her desk drawer with earlier letters. She vowed to keep them forever. David was at his grandfather's, wondering when the next community movie was and hoping they could skate on the pond soon. He closed with lots of kisses and signed the letter Love, David. She answered it that night.

The ground hog prognosticator had seen his shadow which supposedly predicted six more weeks of winter. Phyllis could not imagine how a woodchuck, which was what they called ground hogs in Perryville, could predict the weather. It didn't matter anyway, because winter most always hung around until mid-April.

Some of the gang was sure to show up on Saturday afternoons with brooms to sweep snow off the ice on the pond. It might be Regina, Jimmy V, Florence, Barb, Charlotte, Fred, Wilda, Woody, David, Mary, or any number of country neighbors. The whole gang enjoyed the pond and everyone was welcome. Erwin and Levina did not worry about liability problems.

Wind swirled around thorn apple bushes in the pasture forming circular indentations around the trunks that filled with wet snow; prime raw material for snow balls. It was a good packing day and the kids fired white projectiles at each other, ducking to avoid direct hits.

Phyllis was in seventh grade, Junior High. The gang was growing up, and they did more skating than sliding. As little kids, they prayed for crusty snow. When the weather warmed after a good snow bringing rain during the day and a night freeze, it was the best time for sliding. Getting up early they would slide like the wind all the way from the crest of the hill below the pond back to the barn. They knew how to jump the creek with their sleds sailing over slushy areas where water gurgled beneath the ice.

Snow boulder contests were guaranteed on good snow packing days. Booted, snow-suited, mitten-clad, runny nosed and rosy cheeked, they tumbled single mindedly down the hill in pursuit of huge cascading snow balls that

191

grew enormous as they rolled picking up wet snow. When the snow boulders stopped the kids stopped, too, landing head first in the snow, tossing it, eating it, laughing, care free.

Levina's vanilla custard was waiting in the refrigerator for volunteers to crank the ice cream freezer. A large metal pail held ice, salt, and snow and a second smaller container for the custard fit inside the first. Wooden paddles attached to the cover moved easily at first but got more and more difficult to turn as the custard froze. They took turns grinding the crank and adding more snow and ice as needed. When the ice cream was ready everyone applauded. The rich confection stuck to the paddles when Levina pulled them out of the freezer, and placed them on a pie plate for licking.

Woolen hats and mittens were stacked on the coal stove warming-oven to dry. Little bits of snow sizzled and danced on the hot surface filling the room with the smell of wet wool. Boots were kicked off behind the stove, jackets hung by twos and threes on sturdy hooks and happy kids sipped thick hot chocolate topped with fresh whipped cream, along with homemade ice cream and cookies.

Levina signed up with Madison County Welfare Service for short-term care of three foster children that winter: Barb, Tommy and Joey. At age 15 Barbara was grown up and had a boyfriend back home. She and Phyllis hit it off, but the boys were another story. Joey and Tommy from Oneida were the same age, around 10, not related. Phyllis resented having so many kids in the house, not that it was any of her business. She kept her regular bedroom and Barb got the small room.

Erwin set up a double bed in the big attic for the boys. A full-size window facing the barn let in a modicum of daylight and the unfinished room with its slanted roof and open beams was cozy. The stove pipe from the kitchen passed through the attic room giving off warmth.

The boys were always fooling around which amused Donna but annoyed the older girls who weren't afraid to say so. Levina wrote Phyllis notes asking her not to be so bossy to the boys. Phyllis retorted that they did not behave. Joey had a disgusting problem.

"He pissed the bed again," Tommy whined dropping smelly, wet sheets on the kitchen floor.

"Get those disgusting things out of here," Phyllis yelled. She hated boys. "Take them outside. I am sick and tired of that smell."

Cute, blond Joey hung his head and pouted. Tom punched him. "Piss pants, piss pants

"Stop it," Levina said, "That's enough."

Phyllis was walking up the stairs to bed that night when she thought of it. Why not wake Joey up and have him pee in the pail. The boys had been in bed for a couple of hours already. Maybe he could go.

She tapped Joey on the shoulder whispering his name.

"Get up and pee," she said, "so you won't wet the bed."

Joey was half asleep and he was not shy about peeing in the pail in front of Phyllis. Getting him up nightly kept the bed dry. She didn't turn her head because she was curious. Boys made rude comments about girls' bodies but she and her girlfriends did not talk about boys' private parts. It was the first time she had seen a naked boy except in pictures. She had been too embarrassed to look at her uncle when he exposed himself. Betty had brothers and bare naked boys were not a novelty to her. Betty said their hired man slept naked, and some time when they were having a sleep over she would prove it.

"Not again," Erwin complained every time the family was served a winter salad.

"Practice makes perfect," said Levina.

Phyllis competed at club level and advanced to Madison County Demonstration Day in Morrisville on April 9. Practice did make perfect and the happy young lady won a blue ribbon for first prize and the chance to compete at District Level on May 21.

"I got a blue ribbon, a blue ribbon," she announced when she got home, "first prize." Erwin groaned in anticipation of still more winter salads.

Phyllis was the only participant from Madison County at District competition. Betty went along for moral support. She won another blue ribbon and was one of eight delegates statewide selected to compete at the New York State Fair on September 7.

"Not bad for a beginner," Erwin said with pride.

Phyllis woke up on her birthday feeling ecstatic. She imagined newspaper headlines, *April 21, 1949 – Local Girl turns Thirteen.* She went to school as if it were a perfectly ordinary day and not the momentous occasion she imagined. She would only become a teenager once. Friends brought cards to school. David gave her a pretty box of hankies that she tucked away in her "Forever Box." (*She still has them*). Levina made a butter cake with chocolate frosting for dinner—her favorite.

"Happy Birthday, happy, happy birthday," Donna screeched, grabbing her big sister around the legs.

"You're getting old, Babe," Erwin said. "Is that a gray hair I see?"

"You're not a little girl anymore," Levina said wistfully. "My first born is growing up."

Phyllis opened her gifts after supper. She got clothes. She always got clothes.

Phyllis was an active and outspoken member of the Methodist Youth Fellowship (MYF) that met every

Sunday night at the church. The group members had selected her to attend the annual convocation and her suitcase had been packed for days. Getting out of town was a thrilling event that Phyllis rarely experienced. She was beyond excited on the day after her birthday when she traveled to Penn Yan as Perryville Church delegate to the MYF 12th Convocation.

Erwin said it was 95 miles away on Seneca Lake after he looked it up on a road map. The total cost of the convocation that began Friday noon and ended Saturday evening was $3.50. The fifty cent registration fee was paid in advance. All meals except Saturday breakfast were at the church. Perryville Church paid conference expenses. In return, Phyllis was expected to give a report at the next MYF meeting.

She was ready and waiting when the pastor picked her up for the ride to Penn Yan. She was excused from school and she was leaving town. "Cruising Down the River," was playing on the car radio. She was ready for an adventure, humming to calm her nerves, wondering if she would meet any cute boys.

Phyllis does not remember the worship services, the discussions, or the speakers that are listed on the program that she pasted in her scrapbook. What she does remember is being assigned to stay overnight at the home of Mr. and Mrs. Middlebrook who were members of the Penn Yan congregation. It was not fun because she had to sleep in the same bed with a girl who was a perfect stranger. She cannot recollect her roommate, actually bedmate, but she recalls sleeping as far on her side of the mattress as she could possibly get without falling off. The sleeping predicament was not part of her official report.

Erwin's farm equipment had worn a rough dirt trail up the center of the farm to the top of the hill. Phyllis and

Tommy discovered it made a terrific racing trail for their bikes although not without the threat of peril. They risked their lives day after day racing down the hill avoiding stones with their front tires wobbling. Somehow they made it to the finish line near the barn breathless and unscathed. Levina had not noticed them careening down the hill or she would have put a stop to such dangerous activity. If Erwin noticed he did not say anything but he was more likely to mind his own business anyway. After their chores every day, unless it was raining, they pushed their bikes to the brink of the hill and took off like race drivers down the rutted hill.

"You'd better watch out," Barb cautioned, "or you'll be casualties." Of course they just laughed and the high-speed races continued.

Edna hosted a cosmetic party that summer, and Phyllis stayed over with Betty. The girls gathered free samples of make up after everyone left and headed to Betty's pretty upstairs bedroom. The room had knotty pine paneling on the walls, a flowered chintz dressing table with matching curtains, and bed spreads on the twin beds. Phyllis's room was a hodgepodge of old furniture that didn't even match. She could only dream about a room like Betty's.

Dinah Shore's hit record "Faraway Places," was playing on the radio while Phyllis and Betty took turns sitting at the dressing table on the hot July evening applying makeup. They could not get the mascara right no matter how hard they tried. Phyllis did not have any experience with such things. Levina was not into cosmetics. She powdered her nose and applied a modicum of lipstick when she went out but that was the extent of her makeup.

"Faraway Places," Phyllis hummed, "over the sea….are calling, calling me."

A late night visit to the hired man's room was on their minds as they applied eye shadow and foundation, rubbed it off with cold cream and tried again. Betty was going to prove that the "hunk" hired man slept naked.

They heard him come up the creaky stairs and waited an hour or so before tiptoeing through the dimly lit stiflingly hot hallway to his bedroom located at the far end of the second floor. Light from an outdoor bulb mounted high on a pole pierced the darkness as they tiptoed to the side of the bed where the young man was sprawled out sound asleep. He was all arms and legs and glistening, tanned muscle against white sheets and sure enough, stark naked.

"Can you see?" Betty whispered. Phyllis stared at the naked man for a few seconds until he moved in his sleep. Startled, the girls nearly fell over each other scrambling to make their get-away. Floor boards squeaked and they giggled all the way back to Betty's floral chintz bedroom. It was a wonder they did not wake up the whole house. They collapsed on the beds laughing like idiots.

"Did you see anything?" Betty asked.

"I think so," Phyllis said, but she wasn't sure what she had seen.

"Do you remember when we were little watching your father's bull messing around with the cows?" Phyllis asked, not knowing why she had just thought about the incident. "It was the first time I had seen a bull in action. We were sitting on the stone wall near the pasture looking for fossils in the rocks when the bull made his move and scrambled on the back of a heifer. Do you remember? I was afraid he was hurting her and you, being much more worldly than I, said that's the way calves are made. What a surprise when his peter disappeared inside her, I wondered what the heck they were doing. Boy was I confused."

"Do you understand it now?" Betty asked giggling.

"Yeah, I understand; my mother gave me a book to read. What bothers me is thinking about my parents doing it. Yuck."

"Me too." Betty said.

Levina's contract with the county for foster care ended in August. Evidently whatever problems the kids' parents had were resolved. On the day they were to leave, Phyllis and Tommy took a last bike ride down the farm trail. The ride was daredevil, hair raising, heart pounding fun. They held on tight to the handle bars leaning into the wind as the hay field sped past. In a split second all that changed as Phyllis's front wheel hit a rock and she was catapulted over the handle bars. The bike stopped, but her body accelerated scraping along the jagged dirt path hands first. She hobbled the rest of the way to the house as walking wounded reporting to the kitchen for first aid. It was not the way they had planned the last ride.

"Some people never learn," Levina said in frustration as she cleaned and bandaged her daughter's wounds. Her bike was left on its side half way down the hill.

The welfare worker arrived to pick up the boys as Phyllis walked outside sporting several new bandages. Tommy and Joey looked forlorn standing under the old maple tree with their suitcases. Levina promised to write. Barbara left the next day for Oxford where her mother lived. She hugged Phyllis. "I'll write," Levina said. And, of course, she did. *Two years later they attended Barbara's wedding in Oxford.*

Phyllis enjoyed having the house back to normal. The Lambert's day to day home life was not marked by anger and fighting. Erwin and Levina did not raise their voices against each other. Phyllis could only remember one time when her father got angry and wouldn't come to the supper table. It was her mother's birthday.

"What's wrong?" Phyllis asked after her father dashed out of the house in a huff slamming the door.

"Oh," Levina said with a grimace, "watching the bull gives your father ideas. I was tired, and he didn't get his party last night."

Party? What party? Phyllis thought. She didn't understand, but she didn't ask any more questions because her mother was crying.

"Just like a man," Levina said wiping her eyes.

"I'll get the cake," Phyllis left the table to light candles on the cake she had made for her mother. She guessed her father would have his piece of cake later.

Erwin, Levina and Donna left home after breakfast on September 7, to arrive at the State Fair in time for Phyllis's Winter Salad demonstration. The demonstrations were held in a room with a kitchen on the stage. Rows of chairs at odd angles were set up for spectators. The judges wore serious expressions. Phyllis was nervous. Levina smiled and Donna squirmed in her chair. Erwin leaned forward trying his best to give his daughter's performance his full attention. Of course, he knew it by heart.

It was a larger venue than before, and Phyllis was unusually nervous. Her voice shook and she just wanted it to be over with. In the end she received the award of merit. She was disappointed beyond description with her lack-luster performance.

Miss Young, Assistant 4-H Agent, said just getting to the Fair was an honor. Her effort was reported in the newspaper.

For the first time since 1941 Madison County 4-H members were represented at the State Fair. Outstanding among those to exhibit was Phyllis Lambert from the Adventurers 4-H Club of Fenner. She competed with the best vegetable foods demonstration of the State on September 7 for the State Title. Her demonstration "A Winter Salad" received an award of merit.

Phyllis won many prizes through excellent 4-H club work over the years; the most exciting being an all-expense paid trip to New York City in 1951, and two appearances on Syracuse television stations performing cooking demonstrations.

Later on the family strolled through the extensive fair grounds looking at exhibits. Phyllis took Donna on the Merry-Go-Round. After the ride they got ice cream. Levina and Donna rested on a bench in the park licking their cones. Levina had her favorite maple walnut and Donna had chocolate.

Erwin and Phyllis walked back down the midway because Phyllis had teased to see the freak show. Sights, sounds and smells collided; everyone talking at the same time; do this, see that, eat here, burgers, hot dogs, sausage, onion and pepper sandwiches, drink beer, drink soda, eat popcorn, sweet corn, and ice cream.

Erwin said it was highway robbery because, once inside the tent, they had to pay extra to see the featured attraction. The man on display had a fully clothed Siamese twin brother the size of a baby attached by its neck to the man's belly. Phyllis felt sorry for the man and the baby who had a body but no head. Walking back past the rides, games and food vendors, Phyllis felt dizzy as though she had spun around in a circle. Rides whirled and churned, barkers hawked their wares, and groups of gawking men congregated in front of a stage where nearly naked women enticed them to experience "Mysteries of the Harem" inside their tent.

Phyllis hated to leave the festivities behind, but, as always, the herd of old bolognas was waiting. Phyllis sat reflectively on the ride home trying to recall every detail of their midway walk.

When school began David was in seventh grade, and they attended the same school again. He slipped Phyllis a note the first day when he saw her in the hall. He had a plan worked out for passing notes.

Now that they were both in Junior High, they saw each other nearly every day in the hall between classes. They made plans to stay after school for sports, clubs or music events. Phyllis said she could pretend she was working in the library. David played the trumpet. When they stayed late, they rode home on the 5 o'clock bus that made one stop in Perryville at the school-house intersection.

Dear Phyllis,
My locker number is 53.  *Every noon hour I will put a note in it and you can get it on your noon hour. I'm not mad because you sat with E.L. on the bus because I sat with G.B. I love you very much. Love, David*
P.S. I will put one in tomorrow and you read it and write me an answer FWAK (folded with a kiss)

David's system worked well and they wrote many notes that year. Of course, true love never runs completely smooth, so they say, and every now and then either David or Phyllis got angry for a day or two but their spats didn't last.

The Lamberts arrived early every single Sunday at the small white church that had stood like a sentinel in the center of Perryville since 1839. Just inside the vestibule, a young man rang the bell by repeatedly pulling and releasing the rope that hung down from the belfry.

Phyllis tried to pay attention during the service but her mind wandered to a livelier world of her own. She leafed through the hymnal playing a silent game she and Betty had discovered. Flipping through the pages she looked for facing hymns whose titles formed a phrase. Their favorite duo was Behind the Clouds – What Did He Do?

Uncle Harry had installed the sanctuary wall board squares in tones of beige and cream three years earlier. Her parents had no idea that the walls reminded Phyllis of that terrible day when he insisted she walk with him up the long hill to the pasture pond. She was still scared to death about telling her mother. Certainly her parents would blame her for not running. She wondered about that herself, but at the time, she simply couldn't move.

"What was wrong with me?" she asked Betty when she told her the story in absolute secrecy. "Why didn't I keep running to the house after he put his hand in my panties?"

Betty patted her shoulder. "It's okay," she said. "He's gone."

The congregation was standing to sing the last hymn before she realized what time it was. Yes, he was gone. He never came back.

Thirteen - 1950

The Lambert Family

The New Year tiptoed in on a mild, spring-like Sunday. Erwin called the beautiful weather a "teaser" because it wouldn't last. Phyllis called it "wonderful." They were both right.

"Let's take a walk to the creek," Phyllis said to Donna, "to give Mommy a rest."

Donna skipped along the edge of the creek in earnest exploration holding the toes of her boots under miniature waterfalls as big sister held on tight to her hand. The bright-eyed little girl made a boot print in the mud along the creek and laughed at her cleverness.

203

"Don't get wet," Phyllis cautioned, "Mommy will be upset if you do."

"Where Bowsie?" Donna asked.

"Bowsie is sick, honey. I'm worried about him."

"Bowsie sick." The little girl parroted her sister's words.

Normally the dearest old dog in the world would have been tagging long (he never left his girls out of sight for long). But lately he spent his time asleep in a pile of straw in front of the cows with his nose tucked into his bushy tail.

As Erwin predicted, spring-like weather in January doesn't last. Five days later there was new snow. Phyllis trudged through deep drifts to the barn after supper to say good night to Bowser. Removing her gloves, she caressed her best friend smoothing his soft fur. She tucked a burlap bag around his body, and stroked his head. Bowser glanced at her with glazed eyes when she rubbed his paws. She walked back to the house with tears stinging her eyes.

A bitter cold January wind howled around the old farm house like a banshee with its frigid breath ruffling filmy white curtains. Rags stuffed into window jambs were no match for the cruel south wind. The house shuddered under strong gusts and loose-fitting windows chattered.

Comfy in flannel pajamas and a chenille robe, Phyllis filled her fountain pen with ink and wrote about Bowser in her journal. Mickey cat cuddled up next to her in a black and white fur ball with one paw resting on her leg. She stroked his head and felt the happy vibration of his purrs. Snow fell and swirled as vehicles on the road cut through the storm with headlights piercing endless whiteness. The sound of tire chains on the road carried into the house in a syncopated rhythm like muffled drums. Every now and then a car drove past with a broken link on a chain adding cymbal accents to the winter melody. A monstrous snowplow roared by shaking the house. One man drove and another operated the wing blade. It was a comforting winter sound. People were out and about. The storm was not winning.

Donna stomped into the living room dressed in her footed "jammies," strutted up to her big sister and gave her a hard kick in the leg.

"Hey you little devil, that hurt," Phyllis said rubbing her leg.

Donna wrinkled her nose defiantly, climbed up on the couch next to her father, and stuffed two fingers into her mouth.

"We can't find Bow," Levina said as she reached under chair cushions looking for the love-worn cloth dog. Donna could not sleep without her Bow.

"Now I'll have a bruise," Phyllis lamented rubbing her leg. Donna would never understand about her sister's tender skin disease because her skin was normal. When Erwin changed positions to cuddle Donna he found Bow hiding. Obviously he had a sense of humor which was quite remarkable for a cloth dog.

"I'm worried sick about Bowser," Phyllis said when Levina came back into the living room after tucking Donna and Bow in bed. Erwin had fallen asleep on the couch listening to the popular Bing Crosby radio show.

"I am, too," Levina said, easing her exhausted body into an over-stuffed chair.

Bowser had not come to the house for over a week nor had she seen him frolicking in the snow with Phyllis and Donna.

"He acts exhausted," Phyllis said.

Levina rested her head on the back of the chair and closed her eyes. She was four months pregnant and at 44, had many difficult days during her late-in-life pregnancy. The doctor had advised against another baby at her age, but they were still trying for their son--John Rodney. Phyllis was worried about her health. She prayed that her mother would be rewarded for all her suffering with a bouncing baby boy. She thought blue eyes would be nice too—just like her father's.

A fierce south wind skimmed snow from the tops of drifts in tiny tornadoes on the third day of February— Donna's third birthday. Grandma Hart sent a card with a shiny quarter wrapped in tissue paper. Phyllis would make a cake, but first things first. She had to check on Bowser. She changed into barn clothes after school and walked out the back door. Long icicles stretched from the eaves to the ground like stalactites. Phyllis pounded on the icicles with the snow shovel releasing a booming ice avalanche.

Wading through thigh-high drifts between the house and the barn, icy snow stung her cheeks and clung to her eye lashes. She leaned hard with her right shoulder pushing open the heavy wood barn door that slid sideways on rollers, and pushed it closed behind her.

Erwin's plastic GE radio was jammed between two beams above the cows with the volume turned up. He tuned the radio to Deacon Doubleday's farm show every morning at 5 a.m. Teresa Brewer's hit song, *"Music, Music, Music,"* echoed from the rafters: "Put another nickel in; In the nickelodeon; All I want is loving you; And music, music, music."

Phyllis sang along, "closer, my dear, come closer," enjoying the warmth of the barn and the comfort of the moment. Erwin moved from cow to cow whistling. Milking machines hummed, cats meowed and purred, cows munched hay, slurped water, and contentedly chewed their cuds. Wooden stanchions creaked as cattle stepped side to side, plopped down, struggled up, and relieved themselves; a cacophony blending into a discordant symphony. Phyllis didn't mind the manure smell anymore and she loved the odor of aromatic hay, sweet grist, Lysol, and ointment that Erwin used on cow's teats. The scenario might not sound appealing, unless one loved the place and had no objection to a pungent goulash of odors.

Phyllis walked along the narrow cement walkway next to the last cow in the row to the manger area in front of the cows where Bowser was sleeping. He was in the same place where she had left him that morning. His food had not been touched. Removing her mittens, she caressed his head and his ears and ran her hand down his back. His eyes opened, his tail twitched and he snuggled deeper in the pile of straw that Phyllis fluffed around him. Straw was softer than hay; that was why he had a bed of straw. She nuzzled her face into the ruff of his soft neck fur giving him kisses.

"Poor old pooch," she said "you don't feel very good do you?"

Phyllis could not remember a time in her life when her pal Bowser was not there. He was often her only playmate. They romped in the fields at the farm in Eagle Village when they were both young. He was her body-guard. When Phyllis and her mother left the farm and moved to Chittenango, Bowser went too. He waited by the back stoop until his girl came home from school and slept on the rug next to her bed. She clung to Bowser on the first car trip to the new farm in Perryville. He maintained his watch dog responsibilities, and never chased cars or made a nuisance of himself.

"You're so special," she whispered.

Erwin swept the barn floor between the two rows of Holsteins raising dust and sweeping chaff into the gutter. He stopped to stretch his aching back then came to the manger area where Phyllis knelt next to her dog.

"Bowser is sick," Phyllis said.

"I know, Babe," Erwin said, patting the old dog's head. He couldn't make the dog better. There was nothing else he could say.

Saturday was the only day of the week when Phyllis could sleep late. She enjoyed snuggling in her warm bed keeping the cold air at bay. Donna tramped up the wooden stairs and attacked her big sister with all her little girl might.

"Get up," Donna urged. "Get up! Get up!"

"Stop it you little devil. I'm getting up."

The sisters hurried down the long cold open staircase that ended at the formal front door that no one ever used. Phyllis opened the hall door to the warm first floor letting Donna go ahead. The kitchen was unusually quiet when they walked in. Erwin sat at the table sipping coffee and Levina stood next to the coal range dishing up cream of wheat that she placed on the table. Phyllis lifted Donna into her high chair and sat next to her father. She didn't like the smell of coffee.

"Phyllie," Levina said, hesitating for a second, "Bowsie passed away."

"What?" Phyllis thought about Bowser curled up in the straw the way she had left him the night before.

"No."

"He died during the night," Levina said. "He's not hurting anymore."

"No," Phyllis cried, pushing the cereal away. How could anyone eat? Tears welled in her eyes as she grabbed her coat, slipped into her boots, and ran to the barn hoping her father was mistaken. Passed away? Gone? He had been with her almost forever, she couldn't remember a time when he hadn't been there for her. Gone?

Pushing open the sliding door, she dashed through the barn to the manger in front of the cows. There he was, her wonderful dog, still curled up in a ball under the burlap bag looking peaceful as though he was asleep. For a few seconds Phyllis pretended he was. After all, she thought, death is just another kind of sleep. Sobbing, she curled up in the straw next to Bowser placing her palms gently on his back. His body was cold. It was the saddest day of her life. Nothing would be the same ever again.

Levina and Donna stood quietly and then knelt down next to Phyllis.

"Bowsie," Donna said. "Bowsie dead."

Erwin gently wrapped the old dog in the burlap bag, cradled him in his arms and walked out of the barn. The family followed standing in the wind tearfully watching Erwin place the dearest dog in the world in a grave he had dug next to the silo. The wind had swept a narrow area around the silo free of snow that reminded Phyllis of a manger. Bowser's final resting place was near the barn he loved. Phyllis touched his soft fur one last time, kissed his head, and said good bye. Levina said a prayer for the wonderful pooch who came into their lives when Phyllis was three and passed away when Donna was three. The end of an era.

May was nearly over and spring bulbs were in bloom. The chickens acted happy to be outside, scratching, vigorously, alternating skinny legs left, right, left, right in a chicken boogie uncovering tasty morsels. They grabbed wriggling worms with sharp beaks and swallowed them in one quick gulp. Erwin's herd wandered the pasture free of constrictive stanchions and new kittens appeared.

Levina went into labor on Sunday, May 28. Their friend and former Eagle Village neighbor, Wilda, came to help out with Donna.

"Well, Mom had a girl last night." Phyllis wrote in her diary on Monday morning. "Mom was so disappointed she cried. I could have. I was just mad. Poor Pa, but we'll give him sons-in-law."

Levina was sitting up in bed dressed in a silky pink bed jacket when Erwin and Phyllis walked into the hospital room she shared with three other new mothers. She did not look happy.

"Deborah has the skin condition," Levina announced with a frown and a long sigh. "Her little ankle was skinned when they brought her to me this morning."

Phyllis almost cried. She knew how hard it was having tender skin, and how much each new wound hurt, both physically and psychologically. She didn't want her baby sister to suffer the way she did, but there was nothing she could do.

June 3, 1950, was homecoming for little Deborah Jo. Phyllis had selected her name and she felt very close to her baby sister. She cooked a big dinner for the occasion. Donna was thrilled seeing her mother but not so much the baby. She stared at her chubby little sister then turned away, crawled up on the couch and stuck two fingers in her mouth.

Two days later Levina celebrated her 45th birthday. Family and friends gathered for a double celebration. Debbie was a fussy baby and Levina was exhausted. The baby was not the much-desired boy, but she did have Erwin's pretty blue eyes.

"We tried three times for John Rodney," Levina told everyone who came to the party, "but we got Phyllis, Donna and Debbie."

"We need a new silo, Ma," Erwin said one spring morning at breakfast. "A good swift wind will take the old one down." Levina always resisted large purchases, but after several discussions Erwin prevailed. Levina would need to adjust the budget to squeeze out the necessary money. She held the purse strings tightly.

Erwin and his friend, Clate, trussed up the old silo like a Thanksgiving turkey, and pulled it down with his ancient McCormick-Deering 1020 tractor. The silo split into a pile of boards as it hit the ground with a thundering crash.

Phyllis was excited when three muscular men arrived in a pickup truck on a Saturday morning in June to begin work on the new silo. She sat on the swing under the old maple tree sizing them up. All three were good looking, but one in particular had her attention. Hubba, hubba, she thought, pushing off with her feet to get the swing moving. The swing soared close to the lower branches as she eyed the men.

Room and board was part of the package. Levina made up the double bed and a cot in the guest room. She sighed a lot while she cooked three square meals a day for the ravenous men. She felt over-worked taking care of the house and family including a new baby. She mopped her brow as she slaved over the kerosene stove that was set up in the wood shed for summer use. She stood with her left hand resting on her right side and stirred the gravy with her right hand. She was especially proud of her gravy. No lumps allowed. The mysterious, persistent pain in her right side was back. She saw doctors, but it was never diagnosed. She tried to ignore the pain, but she wanted her family to know it hurt.

A big flatbed truck had delivered curved cement blocks that were piled and ready to go. The men made it look easy the way they fit the heavy white blocks together like building a fairytale tower. Sitting on the swing after school, where she had a good view of the workers, Phyll felt a dizzy sensation watching them climb to the top of the towering silo. They were accustomed to heights and the silo was assembled in a couple of days. Ray, the cutest guy, waved at her from the very top of the silo making her heart race and her imagination soar. She was disappointed when the new silo was finished and the men left for their next job. All good things must come to an end, she thought.

On the heels of the silo men, the Watertown contingent arrived. Erwin's sister Gladys, her husband Ferdinand, their youngest daughter Dona, and her husband Hal, spent a weekend at the farm. They only lived 90 miles away and were frequent visitors. Erwin enjoyed his brother-in-law's company as they worked together and argued politics for most of the weekend. Aunt Gladys was a good helper, although Levina said she was bossy. She liked to fuss with Phyllis's hair, and manicure her nails; things her busy mother didn't do.

The guests raved about the new silo saying it must be nice having lots of money. Erwin countered as he always did about having one foot in the poor house.

Hal saddled up Silver saying he felt like a kid again. Hal acted like a big kid; an obstreperous comedian with a sly twinkle in his eyes. He and Phyllis were buddies. Cousin Dona said it was OK just as long as they weren't "kissing cousins."

Sitting on the lawn while Hal played "cowboy," her cousin, Dona, made a statement that Phyllis didn't understand. "Always remember, "she said, "a man is just a means to an end." It was a long time before Phyllis understood the concept.

Hal returned from his ride pulling up with a flourish like a movie cowboy. Phyllis was eager for her turn in the saddle.

"Hi Hoh Silver, away!" Hal yelled slapping the big horse's rump.

"Thanks Tonto," Phyllis quipped, humming the Lone Ranger's theme song, *The William Tell Overture.*

"Who was that masked man?" Hal shouted as she thundered across the pasture.

Levina stood by the pasture fence with her fingers to her mouth as Phyllis urged Silver to a gallop. "Be careful, be careful." She didn't hear her mother's whisper but she could tell she was praying.

When the crowd sat down for supper, Levina was armed with her trusty fly swatter. Farms and flies were synonymous, although the Lamberts did everything they could to control the pests.

Levina's assault on throngs of flies was intrepid. She swatted constantly and hung fly stickers from the ceiling where disgusting fly corpses stuck tight to the goop. Fly stickers were rolled up tightly in cardboard cylinders until the long, sticky, dark yellow traps were pulled out of the cardboard holder by gripping a piece of string. They were unfurled and attached to the ceiling with a thumbtack (included). Unsuspecting flies landing on the sticker stuck to the surface, wings whirling helplessly. A fly sticker hung directly over the kitchen table with flies buzzing and writhing to free themselves. Their gyrations rarely worked but they died trying.

Levina maintained the "Big Stinky" with a vengeance. The gallon bottle fly trap had multiple one-way entries in the lid. A piece of bloody raw meat was placed in the bottom of the jar along with a solution that she poured over it. It was hung in a tree away from the house and she waited until it filled up with flies--and fill up it did. The excited, buzzing buggers attracted by the rotting meat filled the jar until it was a solid mass of dead flies and maggots. She buried the mess and began again all summer long. She also sprinkled red fly poison granules here and there away from the animals. Erwin sprayed the barn and sprayed the cows. Even the yearly white-washing of the entire cow barn didn't discourage flies. There was no end to them until cold weather returned.

213

The Lamberts' party line phone, 923W, rang on a late Friday afternoon and Phyllis ran to answer it. When the phone rang everyone on the party line could hear a buzzing sound. Nosey people often picked up their receivers to listen in. Phyllis was not entirely guiltless of eaves dropping on a few conversations. She wondered if God included gossip under evil doings but had decided listening to gossip was not a sin. Spreading it was.

"Can you go to the movies?" David asked.

Phyllis was confused. It wasn't community movie night. "When?"

"In Chittenango," he said. "Tomorrow."

"Yes," she said, realizing David was asking her on a date, "sounds like fun." Oh boy, she thought, a real date.

Phyllis floated into the kitchen where her parents were sitting and made the announcement somewhat dramatically.

"I have a date."

"Who with?" Erwin asked.

"David. Who else?"

"That boy always looks like he just stepped out of a bandbox," Levina said. She approved of David. He had a cherub-like smile and neatly clipped light brown hair. He always looked immaculate with clean well-fitting clothes. Levina said he was Little Lord Fauntleroy and Phyllis did not question her mother's wisdom.

"A real date, huh?" Erwin's eyes twinkled, "don't do anything I wouldn't do."

Early on Saturday afternoon Phyllis took a bath, washed her hair, put on a freshly-ironed skirt and blouse and waited.

David's father Ernie drove him to Phyll's house. His mom, Margie, rode along. David came to the door and said hello to Levina and Donna. Debbie Jo was asleep but Phyllis led him to the bassinet to see the baby. David had a sister who was a little younger than he.

David and Phyllis sat in the back seat as Ernie drove down the long hill to Chittenango for the early show. David's parents chatted in the front seat and Phyllis and David chatted in the back seat.

"Stay put after the show," David's dad said, pulling up in front of the movie theater. "We'll pick you up right here."

David bought tickets, popcorn and cokes. Phyllis carried the drinks to their seats.

Movie Tone news blasted on the screen showing an airplane carrying President Truman landing in Washington with the headline: "CRISIS IN KOREA."

"Must be the North Koreans and the South Koreans don't like each other," she whispered to David.

Soon, Phyll's favorite cowboy, Roy Rogers, astride his beautiful Palomino Trigger, and his friends, "The Sons of the Pioneers," were galloping across the screen. Roy and his buddies wore white cowboy hats, shooting at bad guys who wore black hats. At the end of the movie, Roy and the guys rode off singing into the sunset.

David and Phyllis held hands when the popcorn was gone the same way they did at the church movies. It was their first real date and they felt very grown up. There was only one auditorium in the theater showing one movie at a time. It was a double feature, so they got to see two films for the price of one. That day they enjoyed two rooting, tooting, hard-riding, western adventures with cowboys who never got dirty or rumpled. Their first real date was also their last date, although on that day, they could not have imagined such a thing.

After the movies, Phyllis and David walked a few doors up Genesee Street to the Grange Hall. Phyllis and her parents were members of Chittenango Grange, and her father talked about opening a grange in Perryville. He devoted the same amount of enthusiasm and spare time to grange work, as Levina did to church work.

215

They stood on the stoop by the front door of the Chittenango Grange hall while Phyllis briefed David about the grange.   She said the organization helped farmers, but she couldn't talk about secret rituals.

"Maybe you can join my dad's new grange."

"I'll ask my parents," he said.

If Phyllis had a crystal ball, she could have told David that the first meeting of Perryville Grange would be on June 20, 1952, and that her father's grange was very successful.

That summer David's family moved to the town of Nelson located along Route 20, a blip on the map five or six miles to the south.   Nelson was in the Cazenovia School district so no big deal. They would see each other in school. Sometimes they did but it wasn't the same. They no longer rode the same bus, and didn't attend the same church where they passed notes. They couldn't ride their bikes back and forth to each other's homes, walk in the woods or skate on the pond. Saddest of all, they couldn't sit together holding hands during community movies. When they saw each other in the school hall there wasn't time to talk. Notes and letters became less frequent and soon stopped. Phyllis doesn't remember who wrote the last letter.

Their class schedules and the locations of their lockers, undoubtedly contributed to the hiatus. They hadn't seen each other for months, and when they did, it was by surprise. David was standing in front of the school building with friends, and so was Phyllis. When their eyes met it was as though they were strangers. It didn't make sense, but neither Phyllis nor David had anything to say. They simply looked away--forever.

"When are the girls coming?" Levina asked.

"Soon I hope." Phyllis was always the first one ready and anxious to go whenever she made plans with her friends.

You've got time to take care of the pig pail then." Levina kept the pig pail on the back of the kitchen wood stove where potato peels and other edible food waste simmered. Phyllis stopped at the barn and mixed mash with the pig soup that smelled like garbage. She lugged the heavy pail across the pasture to the pig pen that stood next to the creek. Although hogs were instinctively neat and used one corner of their pen exclusively for their toilet, the area was smelly and attracted flies.

The two white porkers wrinkled their long snouts with nasal oinks and snuffling noises when they saw Phyllis who usually fed them. They squealed and grunted jockeying for the best position staring at her with small, beady eyes. She poured the mush into the trough by leaning over the board fence. The eager oinkers got in the way as usual and some of the slop dribbled on their heads and ears. They slurped and grunted making very unsavory noises.

"Hey, you two," Phyllis said, "chew with your mouths closed."

Phyllis moved carefully sideways down the creek bank to wash out the pail and fill it with fresh water for the hogs. Her feet went out from under her on the slippery slope and she slid onto her fanny sitting in the chilly creek water.

"Shit!" She was glad her mother didn't hear her but she was angry because now she would have to change her clothes. She needed to work on her language.

Betty, Mary and Roberta arrived just before 10:00 a.m. with enough supplies to support the Lewis and Clark expedition. Blankets, lots of blankets, pots, pans, food, a shovel and flash lights were loaded on the old blue Radio Flyer-style wagon for their over-night camping trip.

217

A sleep-out in the woods was a dare at first, then a challenge, to find a weekend when all four girls were free of family obligations. They had not intended to wait until late September when the weather can turn on a dime.

A stiff south wind spun dust from the well-worn cow path as they labored up the steep hill along the pasture hedge pushing and pulling the wagon. Maple leaves glowed gold, orange and red in the sunshine.

Phyllis thought about that jerk, Uncle Harry as they walked up the path. She could still smell crushed mint leaves.

"Damn man," she whispered. Betty was the only one who knew.

The girls tied clothes line between two trees, on top of the hill above the pond, and secured heavy, woolen army blankets to the rope with wooden push-on clothes pins. They pulled the heavy blankets to a triangular shape and weighted the edges down with rocks. The camp fire area was ringed with stones supporting a metal oven rack and her mother's large cast iron skillet for frying bacon and eggs. Campfire smoke shifted with the breeze, and when the girls moved, a cloud of smoke followed.

"We'll smell like smoked hams," Phyllis said. "But who cares, were camping."

As teenagers, they felt grown up enough to smoke, and cigarettes were easy to get. Their brand of choice-- Kools was unanimous. Willy, a seductive little penguin, took a cocky stance on posters at cigarette counters promising extra coolness in your throat. It was more than a decade before the Surgeon General's warnings about the dangers of smoking, but they suspected smoking wasn't healthy. They chided older students who regularly walked off school property to smoke.

"Smoke, smoke, smoke, your cigarettes. Smoke, smoke, smoke yourselves to death," they chanted when they saw groups of older teens leave school grounds walking along Caz lake to find a smoking place.

They reasoned that menthol cigarettes were less dangerous than other brands. Indulging their fantasies without detection seemed the riskiest part of smoking. They had one pack between them from a stash hidden in Phyllis's room. They intended to smoke the whole pack and then burn the wrapper.

"Remember when we smoked in your room Phyll?" Betty asked. "What idiots! Your mother yelled through the floor register asking if we were smoking. She must have smelled the smoke, but we denied it. We had the window open, but who did we think we were fooling? Definitely not your mother."

When the camp site was ready they settled down on pillows and blankets around the fire with their smokes and talked about the boys they liked, the girls they did not like, and who had gotten her period.

"I 'came sick' on August 8," Phyllis said.

"Why do you call it that?" Mary asked.

"That's what my mother says. She uses rags that she washes out, and boils on the stove, but she bought me a box of Modess and two sanitary belts."

"The proper name is men-stra-tion," Mary said, mispronouncing the word menstruation. They giggled trying to say the word correctly although no one was sure how it was spelled.

Mary said she beat Phyllis. "My aunt showed me how to use Kotex tampons."

"You're not supposed to use those things before you're married," Phyllis said. "My mother says you won't be a virgin any more if you use them."

Mary said that was silly.

Betty said Phyllis beat her and Roberta, who was a year younger than the other girls, kept quiet.

219

They felt sophisticated beyond description holding Kool cigarettes seductively in their slim fingers. "Keep Kool" the ads said. They acted silly, laughing, trying to inhale, coughing and blowing smoke rings with mixed success throughout the afternoon and evening.

Dusk fell heavy like soot as they finished supper. The sky was barely visible through a canopy of leaves sheltering the grove on the hill above the pond as the wind picked up and grew colder.

The familiar place was scary after dark. Hearing strange noises their imaginations worked over time, and they moved closer to the camp fire. A piece of burning wood snapped; sparks flew. An owl hooted, or at least they thought it was an owl.

"This is spooky." Mary said pulling a blanket tighter around her trembling body.

Lightning illuminated the western sky in sync with simultaneous thunder. Their split-second decision was unanimous

"Let's get out of here!"

Breaking camp and dousing the fire, they pushed and pulled the hastily packed wagon down the pasture hill as lightning streaked across the dark sky and thunder echoed over the hills. They made it to the barn just before the downpour. Pulling the wagon inside the barn near the grain bins, they grabbed their blankets and walked through the dairy barn using a flash light. Cows stirred; their eyes glowing in the light. A cat screeched and ran. They got to the area between the barn and the chicken house and climbed the ladder into the hay mow. Safe at last, they spread their blankets in the hay where they spent a mostly sleepless, itchy night telling stories and listening to rain and hail on the roof.

Phyllis said they had to promise not to tell, but she liked Eddie. Eddie lived on the outskirts of Perryville, but had not attended Perryville School. When Phyllis transferred to Cazenovia Central, and they were in the same class, she secretly admired his devil-may-care, anti-everything attitude. He was fun. Phyllis, too, had a rogue attitude. She couldn't control her thoughts, but, unlike Eddie, she did control her actions.

Eddie watched for Phyllis in the school hallway and pestered her in class. His good looks favored his mother's Italian relatives with sculptured features, a straight, handsome nose and full lips.

Phyllis thrived on male attention. She talked about Eddie at home saying how clever and comical he was. Levina said he sounded like an instigator, and probably best to steer clear of him. Levina was right. Eddie was one of a group of trouble makers who tormented Miss Durkin, the social studies teacher, daily. Tall, awkward and slightly stooped, Miss Durkin was a nervous, flighty spinster who could not control her classes. The instigators lived to disrupt social studies class. They got the word out before class about each planned disruption. At the designated time someone sitting in the front of the room, for instance, would signal and all the students would push books off their desks in a loud, syncopated crash or some other equally disruptive prank.

The principal, Mr. Allen, thought assigning a male practice-teacher to the class would solve the problem. The most riotous social studies class of all was when the student teacher got into a fist fight with the biggest kid in class. They tussled around the room punching and grappling one another, knocking over chairs and bloodying noses as students watched in dismay and delight.

"What about David?" Mary asked.

"My mother says that was puppy love," she explained. Her mother was right, of course, because she had come to think of David as a wonderful childhood friend.

"Eddie's big brother, Bill, is cute too," Mary added.

221

"Yeah, and boring." Phyllis said. "He's so stuck up he never speaks."

Conversation drifted off and they fell asleep in the hay. Phyllis woke up the next morning with a stiff neck.

"Well, look what the cat dragged in," Erwin said when four bedraggled teens, reeking of smoke, walked into the kitchen.

"Don't worry, Ma," he assured Levina the night before as the storm raged, "they're in the barn." He had noticed flashes of light through cracks in the barn siding.

A feeling of panic gripped Phyllis when she noticed a pack of Kool cigarettes on the kitchen table. Her heart pounded and she searched her frantic mind for an explanation to the inevitable question when Erwin picked up the pack and tossed it on the window sill.

"Your friend Edith forgot her cigarettes last night."

"It's a nasty habit," Levina added as she mixed up more pancake batter.

October teased, spoiling everyone with a delightful Indian Summer. They knew winter was not far off, but with such grand days no one wanted to think about snow and cold weather. Phyllis fantasized about an open winter with lots of sun and little snow. She celebrated the season by holding a hayride using Erwin's Farmall-H tractor pulling a wagon brimming with loose hay.

Eugene, Kenny, and Danny, older guys who Erwin trusted with his tractor, negotiated bumpy back roads and the steepest hills they could find. Kids paired off whispering, giggling and snuggling down in blankets nearly buried in hay. The tractor twisted and turned along narrow dirt roads high in the hills above Perryville until everyone except the driver was lost. One man drove while the other two prodded human bumps in the hay making rude remarks.

Hidden under blankets, the riders had no idea they were in Indian Territory as the tractor bounced past Nichols Pond. Local historians claimed the pond area was the site of the 1615 Champlain Battle when Samuel de Champlain, aided by a few Frenchmen and a group of Huron Indians, attacked the Oneida Indian stockade village. It was the site of an archeological dig by Colgate University students who found numerous artifacts, and evidence of post holes where the stockade had stood.

The dirt trail burrowed through bushes and low-lying trees on both sides. Limbs slapped against the wagon prodding kids deeper under the hay unaware of haunted echoes of past battles.

Phyllis was cozy beneath a still-smoky army blanket (although it had been aired on the clothesline) with Eddie who was reciting a Shakespearean soliloquy.

"To be, or not to be, that is the question—Whether 'tis nobler in the mind to suffer the slings and arrows of outrageous misfortune, or to take arms against a sea of troubles...."

The air was brisk and dusty with the fragrance of autumn as the tractor pulled the creaky wagon along the hill country road. Even the man in the moon was smirking. Phyllis felt sorry for the pioneers having ridden all the way out west in bumpy wagons. Eddie had a cute laugh.

The tractor made a sharp left turn, and as headlights pierced the darkness, Phyllis sensed a bright light to the right of the wagon. Sitting up she saw a rustic log house with a huge field stone fireplace perched at the top of the hill in a yard edged with large maple trees. It was illuminated like a movie set by a spot light in one of the trees. A sign in the shape of a rooster nailed on a tree identified the place as THE ROOST.

"Where are we?" Phyllis asked as the wagon trundled on. No one knew.

Phyllis told her mother the cottage was like something out of a fairy tale. "I don't even know where it was."

"Well, neither do I," Levina said as she poured hot chocolate and passed around plates of molasses and sugar cookies. *If Levina had been as intuitive as she claimed, she would have sensed that the cute, hill-top bungalow was where Phyllis and her husband, Bill, would raise their three children, Michelle, Jon, and Aaron. But that's another story.*

"You spent too much money," Levina scolded when Erwin showed up on a November afternoon with a 14 1/2-inch screen Westinghouse television set.

"Naw. The cabinet is solid cherry," Erwin said.

From then on Phyllis and Donna ate supper on TV trays in front of the television set watching black and white western movies. Phyllis fell in love with John Wayne.

Phyllis had watched television in Tyler's furniture store window, and at Betty's house. Betty's family was one of the first families Phyllis knew to have their own television set. Now that the Lamberts had a set of their own, evenings spent around the Farnsworth radio were history. Phyllis remembers three networks: ABC, CBS, and NBC. Programming ended at midnight with the playing of the national anthem. After hours the only picture on the screen was a humming test pattern.

At the end of the first quarter of the school year Phyllis had an F in algebra. Miss Coy, a skinny, hawk-nosed bow-legged "old maid" with tightly permed jet black hair, marched into each math class with high heels clicking on the tile floor, opening every window. When she felt the fetid room was sufficiently aired out, she made a theatrical production of slamming and latching

each window. Phyllis shuddered inside her head. She
was not intimidated by the teacher, but she could not
understand algebra. She disliked math of any kind, but
she despised algebra most of all because it made her feel
stupid. She didn't realize that dropping algebra would be
a defining moment, one that she would regret for the rest
of her life.

(*Having failed algebra, Phyllis didn't feel qualified
to apply for college admission. She left home after high
school graduation at age 18, and moved to Syracuse
where she lived at the YWCA and worked as a secretary
at Carrier Corporation. She took college courses part
time for years, achieving her BA in 2000*).

December snow covered the roads and the meadows
as though nature had spread a layer of baby powder.
Phyllis sang along to the Bing Crosby hit, "It's a
Marshmallow World," as she bundled up her little sisters
in snow suits for a ride on the sled. The air was brisk and
invigorating as Phyllis sprinted, pulling the sled. Donna
supported little Debbie as they shrieked with delight.
Debbie grinned showing five little pearls of teeth.

Phyllis relished her big sister role. She pulled the
girls between tall snow banks along the country road until
their cheeks were as rosy as maraschino cherries. In
frigid weather, electric wires hummed on tall poles like
gigantic string instruments. Phyllis was in a good mood
and she treated her sisters to a long ride, wishing the
whole time that Bowser was there.

It was the day before Christmas, an exciting time at
the Lambert home—the relatives were coming. Aunt
Marie, Kenny and Jerry, Uncle Marinus, Aunt Dorothy,
Wesley and Jackie arrived with baskets of food, bundles
of gift-wrapped packages and a home-made bob sled.
They stomped snow off their boots in the wood shed

entering the cheerful, aromatic kitchen in high spirits. It was Christmas time and they were together.

"We're here you lucky people," Kenny announced, his voice accentuated by boisterous laughter. When Kenny laughed every bit of his body was involved and watching him was contagious--an explosion of happiness.

Uncle Fred, Aunt Marie's husband, didn't attend family gatherings because he was unwavering in his belief that Erwin had broken up Levina's first marriage to his brother George. Actually it was George who had done the cheating, but Fred could not be convinced. Erwin said it was Fred's loss.

"Come on you guys," Jerry urged the kids to hurry. There was no sense in taking off their snow duds when there was outside fun to be had. Kenny and Jerry were anxious to show off their home-made bob-sled. Phyllis helped Donna into her snow suit and boots. Levina said to be careful.

The six cousins trudged across the dormant vegetable garden to the pasture pulling the heavy sled by a rope. They stretched the barbed wire fence high enough to duck under then slogged across the snowy pasture, the frozen creek and snow-covered stone wall into Gerald's pasture across the road from Jay's hill. At the top of the steep hill, they collapsed in soft snow to recover.

All six piled on the sled that was hinged toward the front so they could steer the contraption. The cousins sat with their legs inter-locked for death-defying rides plummeting down steep snow-covered ridges in a chorus of excited shrieks. Phyllis held on tight to Donna. They ended in a heap every time when the bulky sled slammed into a snow bank at the bottom of the hill. There were no casualties. Being bundled up in layers of clothes and thick woolen mittens protected tender skin. They repeated the exercise, pulling the sled up hill and catapulting back down until they were exhausted. Having worked up an

226

appetite, they headed back across the pasture to the cozy house for a delicious meal.

It was the end of an era, but the reality of growing up was not on anyone's mind that afternoon. They were having too much fun. The following winter the bob-sled would be passé when the bob-sled owners moved on to other interests: girls. If the teenagers had realized the simplicity of their lives would soon dissipate into wistful remembrances of their youth, they would have designated one last ride forever after. But they didn't know.

Watch for "Sprigs of Lilacs;"
The Rest of the Story